First World War
and Army of Occupation
War Diary
France, Belgium and Germany

56 DIVISION
Headquarters, Branches and Services
Royal Army Ordnance Corps
Deputy Assistant Director Ordnance Services
5 February 1916 - 30 June 1919

WO95/2939/2

The Naval & Military Press Ltd
www.nmarchive.com
Published in association with The National Archives

Published by

The Naval & Military Press Ltd

Unit 10 Ridgewood Industrial Park,

Uckfield, East Sussex,

TN22 5QE England

Tel: +44 (0) 1825 749494

www.naval-military-press.com

www.nmarchive.com

This diary has been reprinted in facsimile from the original. Any imperfections are inevitably reproduced and the quality may fall short of modern type and cartographic standards.

© **Crown Copyright**
Images reproduced by permission of The National Archives, London, England, 2015.

Contents

Document type	Place/Title	Date From	Date To
Heading	WO95/2939-2		
Heading	56th Division D.A. Dir. Ordnance Services. Feb 1916-Jun 1919		
Heading	War Diary of Major W.S.G. Bishop D.A.D.O.S. 56th Division from 1/2/16 to 29/2/16 Vol I		
War Diary	Croix Du Bac	05/02/1916	05/02/1916
War Diary	Hallencourt	06/02/1916	29/02/1916
Heading	Copy Of A Duplicate Of War Diary Of Temp. Lieut & P.S. Tibbs, A.O.D. D.A.DOS. 56th Division, From 1-3-16 to 31-3-16 Vol 2		
War Diary	Domart	01/03/1916	11/03/1916
War Diary	Doullens	12/03/1916	13/03/1916
War Diary	Le. Canroy	14/03/1916	31/03/1916
War Diary	Le Cauroy.	01/04/1916	30/04/1916
Heading	War Diary of Tempy Captain P.S. Tibbs A.O.D. D.A.D.O.S. 56th Division From 1/5/16 to 31/5/16 Vol 4		
War Diary	Le Cauroy	01/05/1916	07/05/1916
War Diary	Henu	08/05/1916	31/05/1916
Heading	June 1916 War Diary of Temp. Captain P.S. Tibbs. A.O.D. D.A.D.O.S. 56th Division. Vol 5		
War Diary	Henu	01/06/1916	30/06/1916
Miscellaneous	D.A.G. 3rd Echelon	03/08/1916	03/08/1916
War Diary	Henu	01/07/1916	20/08/1916
War Diary	St. Riquier	21/08/1916	01/09/1916
War Diary	Corbie	02/09/1916	05/09/1916
War Diary	Citadel	06/09/1916	30/09/1916
War Diary	Citadel Area.	01/10/1916	06/10/1916
War Diary	Citadel	07/10/1916	10/10/1916
War Diary	Piegnigny	11/10/1916	19/10/1916
War Diary	Hallencourt	20/10/1916	23/10/1916
War Diary	La Gorgue	24/10/1916	31/12/1916
Miscellaneous	Headquarters. 56 Divn "Q" Branch	02/02/1917	02/02/1917
War Diary	La Gorgue	01/01/1917	31/01/1917
Heading	War Diary DADOS February 1917 Vol 13		
War Diary	La Gorgue	01/02/1917	28/02/1917
Miscellaneous	Headquarters, 56 Divn Q Branch	02/04/1917	02/04/1917
War Diary	La Gorgue	01/03/1917	06/04/1917
War Diary	Wail	07/04/1917	08/04/1917
War Diary	Le Cauroy	09/04/1917	11/04/1917
War Diary	La Cauroy	12/03/1917	22/03/1917
War Diary	Beaumetz	23/03/1917	31/03/1917
Miscellaneous	Headquarters 56 Divn Q.	01/05/1917	01/05/1917
War Diary	Beaumetz Les Loges	01/04/1917	20/04/1917
War Diary	Beaumetz	21/04/1917	22/04/1917
War Diary	Souastre	23/04/1917	28/04/1917
War Diary	Arras	29/04/1917	30/04/1917
Miscellaneous	Headquarters 56 Division.	01/06/1917	01/06/1917
War Diary	Arras	01/05/1917	20/05/1917
War Diary	Habarcq	21/05/1917	11/06/1917
War Diary	Achicourt	12/06/1917	03/07/1917

War Diary	Le Cauroy	04/07/1917	23/07/1917
War Diary	Eperlecques	24/07/1917	05/08/1917
War Diary	Reninghelst	06/08/1917	24/08/1917
War Diary	Eperlecques	25/08/1917	30/08/1917
War Diary	Fremicourt	31/08/1917	02/12/1917
War Diary	Fosseux	03/12/1917	04/12/1917
War Diary	St Catherine Arras	05/12/1917	07/01/1918
War Diary	Tincques	08/01/1918	10/02/1918
War Diary	St Catherines Arras	11/02/1918	24/03/1918
War Diary	Bray	25/03/1918	28/03/1918
War Diary	Agnieres	29/03/1918	07/04/1918
War Diary	Montenescourt	08/04/1918	13/07/1918
War Diary	Villers-Sir-Simon	14/07/1918	14/07/1918
War Diary	Roellecourt	15/07/1918	17/07/1918
War Diary	Mingoval	18/07/1918	31/07/1918
War Diary	Montenescourt.	01/08/1918	16/08/1918
War Diary	Ambrines	17/08/1918	21/08/1918
War Diary	Bavincourt	22/08/1918	25/08/1918
War Diary	Bellacourt	26/08/1918	28/08/1918
War Diary	Boisleux au Mont	29/08/1918	07/09/1918
War Diary	St Saveur Arras	08/09/1918	30/09/1918
War Diary	Villers-Lez Cagnicourt	01/10/1918	15/10/1918
War Diary	Mareuil	16/10/1918	30/10/1918
War Diary	Basseville	31/10/1918	05/11/1918
War Diary	Saultain	06/11/1918	06/11/1918
War Diary	Valenciennes.	07/11/1918	09/11/1918
War Diary	Fayt-Le-France	10/11/1918	10/11/1918
War Diary	Blaugies	11/11/1918	27/11/1918
War Diary	Asqvillies	28/11/1918	31/12/1918
Heading	War Diary January 1919 D.A.D.O.S. 56th Division Vol 36		
War Diary	Asqvillies	01/01/1919	31/01/1919
Heading	War Diary February 1919 DADOS. 56th Division Vol 37.		
War Diary	Asqvillies	01/02/1919	28/02/1919
Heading	DADOS 56th. Division War Diary March 1919. Vol 38		
War Diary	Asqvillies	01/03/1919	28/03/1919
War Diary	Jemappes	29/03/1919	31/03/1919
War Diary	Jemappes Belgium	01/04/1919	30/04/1919
War Diary	Jemappes	01/05/1919	30/06/1919

WO 95/2939/2

56TH DIVISION

D.A.DIR.ORDNANCE SERVICES.
FEB 1916 - JUN 1919

War Diary

of

Major W.S.G. Bishop

DADOS 56th Division

From 1/2/16 to 29/2/16
Vol I

Army Form C. 2118.

WAR DIARY
or
INTELLIGENCE SUMMARY.
(Erase heading not required.)

Place	Date	Hour	Summary of Events and Information	Remarks and references to Appendices
Croix du Bac	5/2/16		Left Croix du Bac, having handed over the duties of D.A.D.V.S. 23rd Division to Lt. Meadows C.V.P., and proceeded to Hallencourt to join 56th Division as D.A.D.V.S. Arrived at Hallencourt same day & reported to Head Quarters Division.	
Hallencourt	6/2		Units to form Division not yet assembled, during the day 6 Officers arrived to form part of A.V.C. detachment with Division.	
	7/2		During the day 7 N.C.O.s & men A.V.C. arrived.	
	8/2		One N.C.O. A.V.C. arrived. A.D.V.S. 6th Corps paid visit of inspection.	
	9/2			
	10/2			
	11/2			
	12/2			
	13/2		General Routine duties.	
	14/2			
	15/2		2nd Lt Douglas White arrived for instructional duty.	
	16/2		General Routine duties.	
	17/2		Trucks arrived with first consignment of plates for this Division in exchange for other kinds, also hired for 8 Lewis machine guns to replace Vickers in possession of 1/12th & 1/13th London Regiments.	
	18/2		General Routine duties.	
	19/2		8 Lewis machine guns received for 1/12th & 1/13th London Regiment.	
	20/2		General Routine duties.	

Army Form C. 2118.

WAR DIARY
or
INTELLIGENCE SUMMARY.
(Erase heading not required.)

Instructions regarding War Diaries and Intelligence Summaries are contained in F. S. Regs., Part II. and the Staff Manual respectively. Title pages will be prepared in manuscript.

Place	Date	Hour	Summary of Events and Information	Remarks and references to Appendices
Hallencourt	21/2		Proceeded to H.Q. 8th Corps in connection with formation of Machine Gun Companies.	
	22/2		General Routine duties.	
	23/2			
	24/2			
	25/2		Orders received that Division would hold itself in readiness to move to new destination about 27th. Accepted 2 truckloads of films (moved to H.Q.) pending further orders until notified. General Routine duties.	
	26/2		Moved to Bonnet. Intense frost. Intense Reserves detained in charge of pontoon of rail cars until lorries are available to bring them up. Supply column not yet joined Division. 2nd W. Dragoons told to proceed to 2nd Indian Cavalry Division for duty.	
	27/2			
	28/2		11 Jillho joined this Division for instructions in the duties of D.A.Q.G.	
	29/2		Further, none of Division proceeded for the time being. Horsed transport continuing depôts of units.	

[signatures]

COPY OF A DUPLICATE

OF

WAR DIARY

OF

TEMP. LIEUT& P.S.TIBBS, A.O.D.

D.A.D.O.S. 56th DIVISION,

FROM 1-3-16 to 31-3-16

Secret

Army Form C. 2118.

WAR DIARY
INTELLIGENCE SUMMARY.
(Erase heading not required.)

Instructions regarding War Diaries and Intelligence Summaries are contained in F.S. Regs., Part II. and the Staff Manual respectively. Title pages will be prepared in manuscript.

Hour, Date, Place	Summary of Events and Information	Remarks and references to Appendices
Domart - 1-3-16.	Proceeded to Hallencourt in connection with removal of Reserves	
2-3-16	Established Dump for convenience of Troops drawing stores at Farm La Folie. The 4 Lorries for use of D.A.D.O.S. received from Divl. Supply Column were handed over to-day.	
3-3-16 4-3-16 5-3-16	General Routine Duties. Stores are coming up from Base in very large quantities.	
6-3-16	Dump removed from La Folie to Domart.	
7-3-16	Ordered to proceed to Marieux for duty.	
	(sd) W. Bishop, Major D.A.D.O.S. 56th Division.	

Army Form C. 2118.

WAR DIARY
INTELLIGENCE SUMMARY.
(*Erase heading not required.*)

Instructions regarding War Diaries and Intelligence Summaries are contained in F.S. Regs., Part II. and the Staff Manual respectively. Title pages will be prepared in manuscript.

Hour, Date, Place	Summary of Events and Information	Remarks and references to Appendices
Domart - 8-3-16	Major Bishop proceeded to Marieux for duty. Temp. Lieut. P.S. Tibbs took over duties of D.A.D.O.S. of 56th Division.	P.S.T.
9-3-16	Departmental duties. Received 26 Lewis guns for distribution.	
10-3-16	Received 14700 P.H. Smoke helmets. Arranged with A.A.Q.M.S. as to distribution.	P.S.T.
11-3-16	Received orders to move to Doullens on 12th. Went to Doullens to find a suitable dump.	P.S.T.
Doullens - 12-3-16	Moved to Doullens. Railhead changed from Candos to Bouquemaison Received 40 Vickers guns for Machine gun Companies.	P.S.T.
13-3-16	Colonel Moulton Barrett visited Ordnance Dump. Had instructions to move to Le Canroy.	P.S.T.
Le.Canroy- 14-3-16	Moved to Le Canroy. Owing to accumulation of stores including Vickers guns and P.H. Smoke helmets, nineteen lorry loads were transported. Dump chosen for me is most unsatisfactory.	P.S.T.
15-3-16	Whole day occupied in moving to a new dump owing to the one found for me not being suitable.	P.S.T.
16-3-16	Departmental Duties.	P.S.T.

Army Form C. 2118.

WAR DIARY
INTELLIGENCE SUMMARY.
(Erase heading not required.)

Instructions regarding War Diaries and Intelligence Summaries are contained in F.S. Regs., Part II. and the Staff Manual respectively. Title pages will be prepared in manuscript.

Hour, Date, Place	Summary of Events and Information	Remarks and references to Appendices
Le Canroy – 17-3-16	Visited by A.D.O.S. 6th Corps. Issue of P.H. helmets to Division begun. Vickers guns issued to 167th, 168th, and 169th Brigades.	P.S.T.
18-3-16	Departmental duties.	P.S.T.
19-3-16	Visited by A.D.O.S. 6th Corps. Departmental duties.	P.S.T.
20-3-16	Went to Beaufort to see 1/4th London Regt. re their Lewis guns and also visited A.D.O.S. 6th Corps at Noyelle-Vion.	P.S.T.
21-3-16 22-3-16 23-3-16	Departmental duties	P.S.T.
24-3-16	Went to Doullens to make local purchases	P.S.T.
25-3-16	Departmental duties.	P.S.T.
26-3-16	Visited by A.D.O.S. 6th Corps. Indented on base for second issue of P.H. Helmets for Division	P.S.T.
27-3-16	Departmental duties	P.S.T.
28-3-16	Went to Harbaroq to collect bulged rifles from D.A.D.O.S. 5th Division Called on A.D.O.S. 6th Corps	P.S.T.
29-3-16	Received 15870 P.H. tube helmets to complete Division to two helmets per man.	P.S.T.
30-3-16	Went to Amiens to purchase chairs for Divisional School	P.S.T.
31-3-16	Departmental duties.	P.S.T.

(sd) P.S. Tibbs, Lieut.
D.A.D.O.S. 56th Division.

Certified true copy of a duplicate [signature] Colonel
Woolwich. 1/9/16. Officer i/c A.O. Corps Records.

Army Form C. 2118.

WAR DIARY
or
INTELLIGENCE SUMMARY.
(Erase heading not required.)

Instructions regarding War Diaries and Intelligence Summaries are contained in F.S. Regs., Part II. and the Staff Manual respectively. Title pages will be prepared in manuscript.

Place	Date	Hour	Summary of Events and Information	Remarks and references to Appendices
Auroy	1.4		Departmental duties. 2nd Lt's proceeded to England on leave	
	2.4		Departmental duties	
	3.4		Departmental duties	
	4.4		Departmental duties. Second "P" helmet withdrawn	
	5.4		Departmental duties	
	6.4		Departmental duties	
	7.4		Departmental duties	
	8.4		Departmental duties. Withdrawal of winter clothing commenced	
	9.4		Departmental duties	
	10.4		Departmental duties. ADVS 3rd Army marked & inspected stores & workshops	
	11.4		Departmental duties. 2nd Lt's returned from leave	
	12.4		Routine duties	
	13.4		Routine duties	
	14.4		Routine duties	
	15.4		Routine duties	
	16.4		Went to Arras 15th delivery of mange patches from Depot Potters	
	17.4		Made local purchases in Arras for convalescent ration.	
	18.4		Routine duties	
	19.4		Routine duties	
	20.4		Visited by ADVS & left who inspected Depot. In the afternoon visited mucoin casualty clearing station arranged for normal supply & evil convener dept.	

Army Form C. 2118

WAR DIARY
or
INTELLIGENCE SUMMARY.
(Erase heading not required.)

Instructions regarding War Diaries and Intelligence Summaries are contained in F. S. Regs., Part II. and the Staff Manual respectively. Title pages will be prepared in manuscript.

Place	Date	Hour	Summary of Events and Information	Remarks and references to Appendices
St Sauveur	21/4/16		Departmental duties.	
"	22/4/16		Departmental duties. Visited 8 Middlesex Regt for Board of Survey.	
"	23/4/16		Departmental duties.	
"	24/4/16		Departmental duties. Visited 2/2 London Field Ambulance for Board of Survey.	
"	25/4/16		Visited A.D.M.S. & H.Q. of D.D.M.S. 3rd Div.	
"	26/4/16		Departmental duties. 14,000 P.H. Helmets received in part of Divisional Reserve	
"	27/4/16		Visited D.A.D.V.S. & drew rations 50 short of the from him. Received 2,300 P.H. Helmets in completion of Divisional Reserve	
"	28/4/16		Departmental duties.	
"	29/4/16		Major Meads R.A.V.C. paid a visit of inspection	
"	30/4/16		Visited D.A.D.V.S. & drew rations & drew 60 short after from him.	

J. Lilly Reed
D.A.D.V.S.
56th Division

War Diary
of
Temp. Captain P.H. Sibbs A.O.D.
D.A.D.O.D. 56th Division
From 1/5/16 to 31/5/16

Army Form C. 2118.

WAR DIARY
or
INTELLIGENCE SUMMARY
(Erase heading not required.)

Instructions regarding War Diaries and Intelligence Summaries are contained in F. S. Regs., Part II. and the Staff Manual respectively. Title Pages will be prepared in manuscript.

Place	Date	Hour	Summary of Events and Information	Remarks and references to Appendices
El Ourmy	1/5/16		Departmental duties. Visited A.D.D.S. 6th Corps. Handed over 301 Box respirators to 6th Corps Troops.	
"	2/5/16		Departmental duties. Handed over 51 Vermoral Sprayers to 6th Corps Troops.	
"	3/5/16		Visited Henu to find Ordnance Dump.	
"	4/5/16		Departmental duties.	
"	5/5/16		Departmental duties.	
"	6/5/16		Received orders to prepare to move Ordnance stores to Henu. Sent on Portion gators to prepare Ordnance.	
"	7/5/16		Stores etc being sent to Henu.	
Henu	8/5/16		Whole day spent in moving to Henu. 14 lorry loads of stores transported.	
"	9/5/16		Visited Colonel Hannah A.D.O.S. 7th Corps. Read of Fallen & Bruymesson.	
"	10/5/16		A.D.O.S. 7th Corps inspected Dump & Divisional ships attached exposure of designation of Corps.	
"	11/5/16		Departmental duties.	
"	12/5/16		Made local purchases in Doullens.	
"	13/5/16		Departmental duties.	
"	14/5/16		Departmental duties.	
"	15/5/16		Went to 7 Corps H.Q. Visited Lieut Major & Madison.	
"	16/5/16			

Army Form C. 2118.

WAR DIARY
or
INTELLIGENCE SUMMARY

(Erase heading not required.)

Instructions regarding War Diaries and Intelligence Summaries are contained in F. S. Regs., Part II. and the Staff Manual respectively. Title Pages will be prepared in manuscript.

Place	Date	Hour	Summary of Events and Information	Remarks and references to Appendices
Henu	17/5/16		Departmental duties	
	18/5/16		Departmental duties	
	19/5/16		Went to Southern trench mortars	
	20/5/16		Departmental duties	
	21/5/16		Departmental duties	
	22/5/16		Went to Mortars. Made sundry purchases	
	23/5/16		Departmental duties. Received 12 trench mortars for 167/2, 163/2 & 167/1 & M Betham	
	24/5/16		Departmental duties	
	25/5/16		Went to G.O.D. & got tight	
	26/5/16		Collected & sent in lot from O/o Brewer. Lieut Smith inspector of Armourers worked workshop	
	27/5/16		Departmental duties	
	28/5/16		Received 26 Lewis guns to complete Infantry Batt'n to 8 guns per Batt'n	
	29/5/16		Went to American Armies secondary workshops	
	30/5/16		Departmental duties. A.D.O.S. 2 Corps inspected during forenoon.	
	31/5/16		Departmental duties.	

31/5/16

Original Vol 5

June 1916
War Diary
of
Temp. Captain P.S. Tibbs A.O.D.
D.A.D.O.S. 56th Division.

Army Form C. 2118.

WAR DIARY
or
INTELLIGENCE SUMMARY
(Erase heading not required.)

Instructions regarding War Diaries and Intelligence Summaries are contained in F.S. Regs., Part II. and the Staff Manual respectively. Title Pages will be prepared in manuscript.

Place	Date	Hour	Summary of Events and Information	Remarks and references to Appendices
Heuru	1/6/16		Departmental duties. Fired 1 Box for O&F 4.5 inch Howitzer made no without fittings or carriages, required further one consignment for issue by 4.2.0 m belonging to D. Battery 282nd Brigade.	
	2/6/16		Departmental duties.	
	3/6/16		Departmental duties. Visited by A.D.O. 7th Corps.	
	4/6/16		Departmental duties. Received 4.5" Howitzer for D. Battery 282nd Brigade. Also received 1869 D.H.G. blanks from 37th Division.	
	5/6/16		Departmental duties.	
	6/6/16		Departmental duties. Colonel Walker visited works, seemed very impressed, not satisfied with what he saw.	
	7/6/16		Made total provision in southern.	
	8/6/16		Departmental duties. Attended conference at Hqrs G.A.D.D. 7 Corps.	
	9/6/16		Departmental duties.	
	10/6/16		Departmental duties.	
	11/6/16		Departmental duties.	
	12/6/16		Departmental duties. Visited by A.D.O. 7th Corps.	
	13/6/16		Departmental duties.	
	14/6/16		Departmental duties. Completed equipment of Infantry Battn with wire cutters.	
	15/6/16		Departmental duties.	
	16/6/16			

Army Form C. 2118.

WAR DIARY
or
INTELLIGENCE SUMMARY
(Erase heading not required.)

Instructions regarding War Diaries and Intelligence Summaries are contained in F. S. Regs., Part II. and the Staff Manual respectively. Title Pages will be prepared in manuscript.

Place	Date	Hour	Summary of Events and Information	Remarks and references to Appendices
Albert	19/6/16		Departmental duties	
"	20/6/16		Departmental duties	
"	21/6/16		Departmental duties. Visited by A.D.O.S. 7th Corps	
"	22/6/16		}	
"	23/6/16		} Departmental duties	
"	24/6/16		}	
"	25/6/16		Received twelve 2" trench Mortars from JO 2nd Corps Troops	
"	26/6/16		Received two 2 m trench Mortars from JO 7th Corps Troops	
"	27/6/16		Departmental duties	
"	28/6/16		Received 96 Box Respirators. Visited A.D.O.S 7th Corps	
"	29/6/16		Received 492 Box Respirators	
"	30/6/16		Balance of Box Respirators received in completion of demands of Division. Demands (Kerr-Jones from Gas) Respirators in 2nd reserve by 2nd Linc. Regt.	

J.J. Tibbs Capt.
D.A.D.O.S.
36 Division

D.A.G. 3rd Echelon

Confidential

I enclose War Diary for the month of July 1916.

V. E. WARD Lt.
D.A.D.O.S.,
56th Division

3/8/16.

Army Form C. 2118.

WAR DIARY
or
INTELLIGENCE SUMMARY
(Erase heading not required.)

of D.A.D.O.S. 56 Division. Confidential

Instructions regarding War Diaries and Intelligence Summaries are contained in F.S. Regs., Part II. and the Staff Manual respectively. Title Pages will be prepared in manuscript.

Place	Date	Hour	Summary of Events and Information	Remarks and references to Appendices
Steen	1/7/16		Received Lewis gun for 2nd London Regt from Abbeville	
"	2/7/16		Demanded five Lewis guns for 13 London Regt to replace others lost in action	
"	3/7/16		Demanded six Lewis guns for 18 London, one for 12 London, six for 9 London, eight for 5 London to replace others lost in action. Received four Lewis guns for 13 London Regt	
"	4/7/16		Demanded one Lewis gun for 16 London Regt to replace other lost in action. Colonel Moretto Bennett visited Dump this morning.	
"	5/7/16		Demanded five Lewis guns for 14 London Regt & 5 two guns for 4 London Regt to replace others lost in action. Also five Vickers guns for 169 Brigade Machine Gun Coy and three for 168 Brigade Machine Gun Coy. Received Lewis guns demanded for 5 London, 8 London, 12 London.	
"	6/7/16		Demanded three Lewis guns for 2nd London Regt to replace others lost in action. Received Lewis guns demanded for 9 London & 16 London.	
"	7/7/16		Departmental duties	
"	8/7/16		Received Lewis guns demanded for 2 London & 14 London & London Regt. Also received Vickers guns for 165 & 169 Bde Machine Gun Coys	
"	9/7/16		Departmental duties	
"	10/7/16		Inspection salvage Dumps at Pos. Hasleby & Sceno.	
"	11/7/16		Took over 2 Stokes Mortars & 2 S.M. Shelley for inspection. Visited by ADOS 167.	
"	12/7/16			
"	13/7/16		Demanded 5 they [?] Lewis guns [?] for 169 S.M. Battery & one for 167 S.M.B. to replace others lost in action.	

Army Form C. 2118.

WAR DIARY of D.A.D.O.S. 56th Division.

INTELLIGENCE SUMMARY

Confidential

(Erase heading not required.)

Instructions regarding War Diaries and Intelligence Summaries are contained in F. S. Regs., Part II. and the Staff Manual respectively. Title Pages will be prepared in manuscript.

Place	Date	Hour	Summary of Events and Information	Remarks and references to Appendices
Heuou	14/7/16		Demanded one 3" Stokes trench mortar for 168 T.M. Battery destroyed by shell fire	
"	15/7/16		Received 9 trench mortars demanded on 13th inst for 167 & 169 T.M. Batteries. Also a 2nd 9 get lots of General personal instructions stores of the 37th Division Army which has been left with many barrow items.	
"	16/7/16		Received 1 trench mortar for 166 T.M. Battery. Busy closing up 37th Div. Trnsp.	
"	17/7/16		Departmental duties	
"	18/7/16		Departmental duties	
"	19/7/16		2nd Lieut U.B. Hare joined for duty	
"	20/7/16		Departmental duties	
"	21/7/16		Departmental duties	
"	22/7/16		Conferred with taking over of duties as D.A.D.O.S. from Temp. Capt. P.S. Titts	
"	23/7/16		Temp. Capt. P.S. Titts left for duty at Marseilles	
"	24/7/16		Departmental duties	
"	25/7/16		Departmental duties. Went to Amiens for local Purchases (Brushes)	
"	26/7/16		Departmental duties. L.d. Grant selected. L.d. Warwick selected. Inspected dump	
"	27/7/16		Departmental duties	
"	28/7/16		Inspected ammunition salvage dump	
"	29/7/16		Departmental duties	
"	30/7/16		Visited Rivilland (Burgomaster) Souastre, Bienvillers, St Amand - Departmental duties	
"	31/7/16			Keusard Lt. 56th Division D.A.D.O.S. 31/7/16

Sheet 1
Army Form C. 2118.

Confidential — August 1916 —

WAR DIARY
INTELLIGENCE SUMMARY

(Erase heading not required.)

D.A.D.O.S. 303 52nd Division

Vol 7

Instructions regarding War Diaries and Intelligence Summaries are contained in F. S. Regs., Part II. and the Staff Manual respectively. Title Pages will be prepared in manuscript.

Place	Date	Hour	Summary of Events and Information	Remarks and references to Appendices
Heron	1.8.16		Visited Divisional Baths & Laundry at Pero. Inspected clothing.	
"	2.8.16		Departmental duties. Visited various units.	
"	3.8.16		A.D.O.S. called & arranged for my office (to be moved to Hd. Qtrs. Artillery.)	
"	4.8.16		Departmental duties. Local Junction at Bailleul.	
"	5.8.16		Instructions to move my office to Hd. Qtrs. cancelled by A.D.O.S.	
"	6.8.16		Visited VII Corps Mobile Workshops.	
"	7.8.16		Departmental duties. Local Junction.	
"	8.8.16		Recd from Base Gums Return 303 (1) Rgt Nos 4428- for 168 M.G. Coy.	
"	9.8.16		Suggested to Hd. Qtrs. the advisability of starting a Divisional Wheelwright Shop in view of the fact that limits of vehicles (shafts, trailers etc) are difficult to obtain from Base. Tent Junction is now experienced without of replacing and stores on our district.	
"	10.8.16		Visited A.D.O.S. Question of 164 outfits for Brigade around.	
"	11.8.16		Departmental duties.	
"	12.8.16		Visited various units. Inspected stores.	
"	13.8.16		Departmental duties.	
"	14.8.16		Departmental duties.	
"	15.8.16		Departmental duties.	
"	16.8.16		Departmental duties.	
"	17.8.16		Departmental duties.	

2449 Wt. W14957/M90 750,000 1/16 J.B.C. & A. Forms/C.2118/12.

Sheet II
Army Form C. 2118.

Confidential

August 1916 — (Continued)

WAR DIARY
or
INTELLIGENCE SUMMARY D.A.D.O.S. 56th Division

(Erase heading not required.)

Place	Date	Hour	Summary of Events and Information	Remarks and references to Appendices
Hmn	18.8.16		Visited Trucks at Longueuillers & other places in rotn to see that Salvage work is carried out properly.	
"	19.8.16		Departmental duties — Preparation for move.	
"	20.8.16		Moved to St. Riquier.	
St. Riquier	21.8.16		Departmental duties.	
"	22.8.16		Moved my office to Hd. Qrs. building — Lack of space offices. caused inconvenience.	
"	23.8.16		Departmental duties.	
"	24.8.16		Departmental duties — Arranged with C.O.O. at Abbeville for the repair of Bodies & other parts of vehicles in Division.	
"	25.8.16		Departmental duties. Local purchases at Abbeville.	
"	26.8.16		Departmental duties — Interviews with D.O.S.	
"	27.8.16		Departmental duties.	
"	28.8.16		Departmental duties. Local purchases at Abbeville.	
"	29.8.16		Selected dumps for Artillery units — Departmental duties.	
"	30.8.16		Informed A.D.O.S. of difficulties in performing certain duties such as visiting units & inspecting stores, owing to the fact that all cars are pooled in the Division & Staff were not always anything anyone wants a car.	
"	31.8.16		Preparations for move.	

Edward [?]
D.A.D.O.S.
56th Division

Sheet 1

WAR DIARY
or
INTELLIGENCE SUMMARY

Army Form C.2118

D.A.D.O.S. 56th Division

Place	Date	Hour	Summary of Events and Information	Remarks and references to Appendices
St. Riquier	1/9/16		Departmental duties & Preparations for move.	
Corbie	2nd		Moved to Corbie. Visited railhead & formed new dump.	
"	3rd		At Corbie. Difficulty experienced in carrying out Ordnance duties in consequence of "Q" Branch not providing a car. I am unable to move without this day.	
"	4th		Smoke helmets & Artillery Stores arrive.	
"	5th		"Q" Branch instructs me to arrange for the return of 12 G.S. Wagons to Base. The wagons, apparently surplus ones, had been retained by the Division but "Q" had not informed me of this previously & much time & labour lost through "Q" not informing me of this matter before the Division commenced to move.	
Citadel	6th	3pm	Moved to Citadel. (F.21.B.) Formed new dump.	
"	7th		Departmental duties. Applied to "Q" for telephone as dump is situated at a considerable distance from Hd. Qrs. Telephone promised.	
"	8th		Telephone not to be supplied. Departmental duties.	

Confidential.

September 1916 — Sheet II

WAR DIARY or INTELLIGENCE SUMMARY

(Erase heading not required.)

D.A.D.O.S. 56th Div

Army Form C. 2118

Instructions regarding War Diaries and Intelligence Summaries are contained in F. S. Regs., Part II. and the Staff Manual respectively. Title Pages will be prepared in manuscript.

Place	Date	Hour	Summary of Events and Information	Remarks and references to Appendices
Citadel	9/9		Local purchase of Calico etc. Departmental duties — Guns etc. demanded Carriage Field 18 Pdr. for A.281 Batty. One Vickers gun for 168 M.G. Coy.	
"	10th		Interview with A.A. & Q.M.G. concerning extraordinary attitude of "Q" Branch towards Ordnance. The attitude of the A.A. & Q.M.G. especially referred to. The A.A. & Q.M.G. promised to speak to the D.A.Q.M.G. in regard to the matter. One 18 Pdr. gun without Breech fittings demanded for C.280 Battery. Two Vickers Guns demanded for 169 M.G. Coy. Visited Main Dressing Station at Billon Farm. Visited A.D.O.S. XIV Corps re Guns etc. One Lewis gun for 5th London Regt.	
"	11th		75 for 9th London Regt. demanded. Asked A.D.O.S. to handle guns.	
"	12th		Phoned A.D.O.S. 7 again asked for guns to be handed following guns demanded this day; Lewis Guns — 3 for London Regt. B; 12th London Regt. 6; 13th London Regt. 1; 4th London Regt. 2; 1x Stokes Mortars 3" — 2 demanded for 169 T.M.B. × Carriage Field 18 Pdr. received for A.281 Batty.	
"	13th		One Lewis gun demanded for 8th Midd. Regt. × Visited A.D.O.S. re Guns T.M. guns etc. One 18 Pdr. Gun rec'd for C.280 Batty. One Vickers Gun rec'd for 168 M.G.C. Eighteen Lewis guns rec'd from X Division to complete above one. Rec'd 2 Vickers Guns for 169 M.G.C. × Rec'd 2 Stokes Mortars 3" for 169 T.M.B.	
"	14th		1 Carriage Field 18 Pdr. demanded for C.282/Batty. 1 ditto for B.a.82 Batty. Visited A.D.O.S. at Meaulte.	
"	15th			

Army Form C. 2118

Confidential. September 1916. Sheet III.

WAR DIARY
INTELLIGENCE SUMMARY

(Erase heading not required.)

D.A.D.O.S. 56th Division

Place	Date	Hour	Summary of Events and Information	Remarks and references to Appendices
Citadel	16th		1 Vickers' gun demanded for 169 M.G.C. 1 T.R. for 167 M.G. Coy.	
"	17th		1 How. 4.5" Carr. demanded for B.280 Batty.	
"	18th		Visited A.O.C.S. & following guns demanded; 8 Mks. 2; 7th Mks. (a); 1st London H; 16th London H; Asked "Q" for car but not available at time required.	
"	19th		Visited A.D.O.S. & Reced 1 Carriage Field 18 Pdr for 6.282 Batt. Reced 1 Vickers' gun for 169 M.G. Coy. One Lewis gun demanded for 1/8 Middx. Regt. Asked "Q" for car but not available at time required.	
"	20th		Reced two Vickers' guns for 167 M.G.C. x Three Lewis guns demanded for 16 Lon. Regt. (This indent reports this gun out of action on 10/9/16 Indent sent to me on the 20/9/16) Car asked for & arrived one hour late. Sefantrated duties. Stores due from Base to day did not arrive. R.T.O. has no information.	
"	21st		Eighteen Lewis guns arrive from Base to be rect to V Division. # D.A.Q.M.G. states that these guns should be returned by us for a few days.	
"	22nd		Sefantrated duties. One Lewis gun demanded for 9th London Regt. How. 4.5" Car. rect for B.280 Batty.	
"	23rd		Visited A.D.O.S. Obtained Carrier Carrier Magazines Lewis Guns 455. Car came for How. 4.5 to be taken from XV Corps 9.O.M.	
"	24th			
"	25th		One Lewis Gun rect for 14th London Regt. Telephoned Tournai A.T.O.S. concerning Lewis gun magazines Ammn.	

Confidential. Sheet IV. September 1916 –

Army Form C. 21

WAR DIARY
INTELLIGENCE SUMMARY
(Erase heading not required.)

D.A.D.O.S. 56th Division

Instructions regarding War Diaries and Intelligence Summaries are contained in F. S. Regs., Part II. and the Staff Manual respectively. Title Pages will be prepared in manuscript.

Place	Date	Hour	Summary of Events and Information	Remarks and references to Appendices
Citadel	26th		Visited Corps Barrage Dump + C.E.S. x Collected Steel Helmets + Lewis Gun mgs for 9th London Regt.	
"	27th		Departmental duties.	
"	28th		Departmental duties + Car not available x	
"	29th		One Vickers Gun required by 1st. Q. M.G. Coy. x Car not available x	
"	30th		Departmental duties.	

I must place on record the following facts + The Ordnance work in this Division is continuous hampered + restricted by the fact that "Q" Branch frequently details the Ordnance lorries for Reinforcements, Musketry Comforts etc. in spite of the regulation laid down that the four Ordnance lorries are for the sole purpose of carrying Ordnance Stores + Clothing. Much inconvenience + delay is caused by the practice in this Division of providing H.Q. Ord. cars. I am entitled to a car by War Establishment but this is taken by Div. Hd. Qtrs. It often occurs that a car is not available when I apply for one.

V. Ward Lt.
D.A.D.O.S.
56th Division

5/10/16.

WAR DIARY / INTELLIGENCE SUMMARY

Army Form C. 2118.

Confidential   October 1916.   SADOS 56th Division

Place	Date	Hour	Summary of Events and Information	Remarks and references to Appendices
Citadel Area	1st Oct.		Departmental duties. Inspected Latrines. Welfare brothel.	Vol 9
"	2nd		Local purchase of cooker urgently needed by Div. to make up delay.	
"	3rd		Accompanied A.D.M.S. to Div. Bath Laundry at Amiens. The present clothing suggested certain improvements in organisation to prevent loss of nothing in clothing collected from Div. till ADS captured during recent advance. Recommended for T & S Meeting.	
"	4th		1 Vickers gun lost for 169 Machine Gun Coy. Urgent indemnances received by "Q" Branch taking away two of my lorries when I acceded the Corps for Disbursement work. Reported the matter to the Division.	
"	5th		Visited A.D.O.S. XIV Corps re Supply R.E. Matron Magazine Games & other important stores. The F.A. Steel modified one of my lorries to go to Amiens with 20 men to commence Laying down Drainage work required by the much increased Policy at Drainage work carried out this period by the action of "Q" Branch in not supplying one with a car on a telephone.	
"	6th		At 10pm I was told that the C in C commanding the office I wished you were of the telephone. He kindly allowed one the use of the telephone of the one and granted me a telephone of my own.	

WAR DIARY or INTELLIGENCE SUMMARY

Army Form C. 2118

Confidential
D.A.D.O.S. 56th Division
October 1916

Place	Date	Hour	Summary of Events and Information	Remarks and references to Appendices
Citadel	Oct 7th		Started for Div. H.Q. Amby car at 5:30am - arrived at 6:30am. Presently an urgent needs of Division coming to H.Q. Officers with DADOS consisted in this function. I naturally asked "Q" Branch for a telephone. It was free promised but is was not supplied. Depended on Division journals to keep Div. dept in touch of Division	
"	" 8th		Reference for mules. Great inconvenience caused by "Q" not supplying mules as allotment. A.D.C., D.S. Mul P. Ambulances etc.	
"	" 9th		Lorries loaded Monday to move to new destinations. Div. Amb. about Normont. The E. a Q.M.G. gave me an order to move as large quantity of clothing belonging to the Div. Bath Train which I had no control. This delayed any move programme. I arrived great inconvenience. I then applied for a motor car to enable me to travel ahead of my lorries to make the necessary arrangements for a new dump. My request was refused by "Q" therefore I was lately travel by lorry. Thus I did travelling all night reached Péronne at 3:30am. I had had no arrangements as dump although no prospect of making fresh arrangements. Dep. at arrival station.	
Péronne	" 11th			
"	" 12th		Interview with A.A. & Q.M.G. in attitude of "Q" Branch towards Division. Reported the matter to the A.D.O.S. the Q.M.G. informed me that I had no fault to find with the conduct of "Q" Branch, shewed that he was disgusted with organisation, that I must be very fatigued I pointed out that I had frequently asked for help in that matter & that "Q" had refused. Accordingly ordered.	

Army Form C. 211

WAR DIARY or INTELLIGENCE SUMMARY

Army Form C. 2118

October 1916

Place	Date	Hour	Summary of Events and Information	Remarks and references to Appendices
Rigny	Oct 12		3 Lewis guns demanded for 2/4 London Regt.	
"	13		Departmental duties. Interview with G.O.C. in regard to reinforcements. Pointed out the absolute need of "Reach" not fired in any batt.	
"	14		A.S.O.S., T.B.O.S. & Only 2 Lewis guns demanded for 4/London Regt.	
"	15		Recommended A/Sub. Lieut. J. Anderson (my Chief Clerk) for 2nd Lt. Observer to admit. Lewis guns demanded: 2 for 14 Lon Rgt.; 1 for 9 Lon.; 3 for 12/Lon Rgt. Lewis guns demanded: 3 for 3/Lon; 2 for 5/Lon Rgt.	
"	16			
"	17		B.T.O.S., X Corps T.O.S.O.S. X Corps F IXI Corps called. Departmental duties.	
"	18		Asked "Q" for ammunition truck. Reply "no not available."	
"	19		Asked "Q" for car to send truck in reply "car not available—attached to Div" transportation. "Q" noted away one of any series although needed of for	
Hallencourt	20		Ordnance truck. Move to Hallencourt. Arranged new dumps. Departmental duties. Lewis guns recd. 2 for 14 Lon; 1 for 9/Lon.; 3 for 12/Lon; 1 for 1/Lon Rgt.	
"	21		Departmental duties.	
"	22		Visited Longpré by Lorry. Arranged for move.	
"	23		Left at 6.30 arrd at 1 Lorry.	

Army Form C. 2118

WAR DIARY
or
INTELLIGENCE SUMMARY

(Erase heading not required.)

October 1916.

S.A. D.O.S. 56th Div.

Instructions regarding War Diaries and Intelligence Summaries are contained in F. S. Regs., Part II. and the Staff Manual respectively. Title Pages will be prepared in manuscript.

Place	Date	Hour	Summary of Events and Information	Remarks and references to Appendices
La Gorgue	Oct 24		Accommodation rented by Surveyor for Ordnance dump found to be inadequate & unsuitable. Saw S.A.D.O.S. 61st Div. & obtained use of some tents –	
"	25		Called at Q — got up arrival —	
"	26		Called at Q – Departmental duties	
"	27		Departmental duties. Called at Q. Unable to obtain a car from my own Division & applied to the 61st Div. who arranged. The rent of a car between A.D.O.S., Cashier & Paymaster settled at £6.	
"	28		Departmental duties. Called at Q —	
"	29		Departmental duties. Called at Q —	
"	30		Departmental duties. Enrolled A.S.C. Attd. for location & take of units & formation Departmental duties. Called at Q — Went down to Lillers Ordnance School for instruction. Lecture by South Lancs with reference to being gas alarmed for instruction. Called at Q — Rode to G.H.Q. for lecture & return late in the evening.	
"	31st		Departmental duties. Called at Q. Proceeded on aerial photography & journey to the Division. Further instructions were made caused by the altitude of W Orders instructing to the north of the S.A. & M Guns in answer to to the Ordnance as soon as possible in regard to anti-aircraft of a carefully important nature – Information sent in that my officers ought to be any sufficient endangering local purchases & would take – have not seen officers long attached of the S.Q.M.S. Sgt. which has been found I established my work.	

WAR DIARY or INTELLIGENCE SUMMARY

Army Form C.2118.

October 1916.

D.A.D.O.S. 5th Division

Late in September I received an order from the A.A. & Q.M.G. to obtain and issue a large quantity of S.D. Clothing. Almost immediately the clothing was returned by units to my store the reasons being that the units could not use the clothing & they were unable to carry same in their transport. This is an instance shewing the difficulties under which the Ordnance is carried out in this Division —

By Army Orders I am entitled to the use of a car. The car has been taken away by Sir T. I have been unable to obtain the use of same on many occasions when I have been in urgent need of a car for the purpose of visiting the A.D.O.S., the D.D.M., men in workshops, railheads etc. — By Army Orders I am entitled to the use of four lorries. I am instructed that these lorries are for the sole purpose of Ordnance Service. The lorries have been frequently taken away by "Q" Branch at times when I have needed them urgently for Ordnance work. The attitude of the A.A.Q.M.G. towards the Ordnance has rendered impossible the co-operation which should exist between the D.A.Q.M.G. & the D.A.D.O.S. — The above Remarks are made in the interests of the Service —

F.C. Ward Lt.
D.A.D.O.S. 5th Division 5/11/16.

Army Form C. 2118.

WAR DIARY
-or-
INTELLIGENCE SUMMARY
(Erase heading not required.)

November 1916

Vol 10

Place	Date	Hour	Summary of Events and Information	Remarks and references to Appendices
La Gorgue	1/11/16		Departmental duties. Ended at 8.15 a.m. & 6 p.m.	
	2/11/16		Packed Adv. Dn. 6 pm. 7 to 9 pm. Departmental duties.	
	3		Departmental duties.	
	4		Departmental duties. Wrote "G" instruction Confidential war	
	5		Departmental duties. "G" instruction re prevention of illicit sound of intoxicants	
	6		Inspected Bakeries. Departmental duties.	
	7			
	8			
	9			
	10			
	11			
	12			
	13			
	14			
	15			
	16			
	17			
	18			
	19			
	20			
	21		Departmental duties. Capt. Hutchinson arrived & took over duties of A.D.O.S.	
	22		Spent the day inspecting stores, workshops &c	

Army Form C. 2118.

WAR DIARY
or
INTELLIGENCE SUMMARY
(Erase heading not required.)

Instructions regarding War Diaries and Intelligence Summaries are contained in F. S. Regs., Part II. and the Staff Manual respectively. Title Pages will be prepared in manuscript.

Place	Date	Hour	Summary of Events and Information	Remarks and references to Appendices
La Bryne	23/11/16		Lieut Ward, from Daddys of this Division, left for duty with 1st Canadian Corps. Group.	G. S. T. A.
"	24/11/16		Passed the day in familiarizing myself of Personnel with the working of Ordnance Services in the Division.	G. S. T. A.
"	25/11/16		In company with D.A.D.O.S. Div visited A.D. Arm. of 137 & 138 Inf. Bdes. Also A. Dn Pioneer Baths (5th Cheshires)	holiday G. S. T. A.
"	26/11/16		A.A. + Q.M.G. of Div visited Ordnance "dumps" various roads in Division.	G. S. T. A.
"	27/11/16		Specially reviewing the administration of Div Ordnance. Superintended Issues.	a. S. T. A.
"	28/11/16		Confer with D.A.D.O.S. and visited H. Qrs of 55 Div Artillery attached.	G. S. T. A.
"	29/11/16		3 → Canadian Div	
"	30/11/16		At Ordnance Dump trying to establish feasible Superintending the administration of Brie.	G. S. T. A.

WAR DIARY
or
INTELLIGENCE SUMMARY

Army Form C. 2118

Shut 1

D.A.D.O.S. 56 D

Vol XI

Place	Date	Hour	Summary of Events and Information	Remarks and references to Appendices
to ffpe	1/12/16		D.A.D.M.S. came to my office & I spent some time in examining various matters connected with the equipment of the Division	6. D.H.
"	2/12/16		Regimental duties occupied me throughout the day. Lieut Dodds enlisted & undergo instruction	6. D.H.
"	3/12/16		A.D.O.S. XI Corps visits & inspects Armt. & workshops & inspires D.M.	6. D.H.
"	4/12/16		interviewing Officers of Armt.	6. D.H.
"	5/12/16		Occupied throughout the day attending to departmental work	6. D.H.
"	6/12/16		Occupied throughout the day superintending work of my department	6. D.H.
"	7/12/16		General interviewing work	6. D.H.
"	8/12/16		Visits to A.D.O.S. XI Corps	6. D.H.
"	9/12/16		Visits to A.A. & Q.M.G. XI Div. also inspects M.O.	6. D.H.
"	10/12/16		Departmental duties occupied me throughout the day	6. D.H.
"	11/12/16		Lieut Dodds left the Division for duty at Canadian Khakers	6. D.H.
"	12/12/16		Owing to the attending DM ammunition & breveting work & department	6. D.H.
			A form of telephone of the making of Ordnance Service in General	6. D.H.

WAR DIARY
or
INTELLIGENCE SUMMARY
(Erase heading not required.)

Army Form C. 2118
Sheet 2.

Place	Date	Hour	Summary of Events and Information	Remarks and references to Appendices
In Joypur	13/12/16		In company with Lt. Col. Sarkar I. Sir visited the Quartermaster stores & office. [illegible] with Lt. Col. [illegible] [illegible] & when guards, picket up accumulated [illegible]. He returns to Johanne	U.S.H.
	14/12/16		Visited with D. Adjt & Supt. the Q. master stores at Namuto Jighat Battalion stores. Lt. Johanne stores were being issued; ordered only to the two battalions accumulation for packing were found on to its shipment for their any accumulation.	W.S.H.
	15/12/16		Passed the day supervising work at Office, & Group Workshops	6 S.H.
	16/12/16		S.Dav. 1st Army visits Group & Workshop & enquiries into the system of administering Ordnance services with Lt. Gen. Bull afternoon visits Ordnance Stores, &	S.H.
	17/12/16		Visits 9 M.G. 193 Machine Gun Co. [illegible] full enquiry as to its Equipments its Equipment & made full enquiry as to its Equipments	W.S.H.
	18/12/16		Occupies the whole day with H. Routine Ordnance work & Div. admin	U.S.H.
	19/12/16		Lt. Col. Saarn of Div. inspects Q. master stores 1 169 Inf. Brigade	W.S.H.
	20/12/16		Spent the day informing into Deficit stores	U.S.H.
	21/12/16		Went to the Sant & Mirville to visit Training Battn formed from taken recruits before joining their respective units. Interviews with Q. master Re. supply matters Re. clothing stores.	6. S.H.

Army Form C. 2118.

WAR DIARY
or
INTELLIGENCE SUMMARY

(Erase heading not required.)

Sheet 3

Instructions regarding War Diaries and Intelligence Summaries are contained in F. S. Regs., Part II. and the Staff Manual respectively. Title Pages will be prepared in manuscript.

Place	Date	Hour	Summary of Events and Information	Remarks and references to Appendices
La Fogue	22/12/16		Brigade in billets with HQ and personal administration of Ordnance with HQ Division	b. D.H.
"	23/12/16		L.H. ADMS visits "Group" workshops, he discussed several matters	b. D.H.
"	24/12/16		Left HQ Ordnance receipt + issue United HQ Divisions Battn + inquired into equipments of Munitions regarding the return of unserviceable clothing to Ordnance	b. D.H.
"	25/12/16		Xmas Day — performed duties	
"	26/12/16		Passed the day attending BM duties, SM Dept + mercury supervision over its working	b. D.H.
"	27/12/16		Occupied with the routine duties of SM Dept	b. D.H.
"	28/12/16		HQ Batt'n A, 2nd & 3rd of SM Div visited by Staff & Workshops; also had a meal for A.D.O.S. II Corps	b. D.H.
"	29/12/16		Routine duties of SM Dept's; also to front into Conference concerning full inspection of SM transport vehicles of different units with Div	b. D.H.
"	30/12/16		Present at inspection of SM transport of Standards by S.O.M.B., ADiv Ar. Bn. A.D.O.S. the reports for supplies for empty Perrin wagons - not following up	b. D.H.
"	31/12/16		Contracts the work of the SM day inspection of transport of units — Passes SM Establishment of SM day inspecting with SM Std Bn Horbm Lgtt + Grades St Bn.	b. D.H.

Confidential

Headquarters
56 Divn
"Q" Branch

Enclosed herewith please find my War Diary for the month of January 1917

D.D. Halburn
Capt
DADOS
56 Divn

D.A.D.O.S.
56th DIVISION
No.
Date 2.2.17

Army Form C. 2118

WAR DIARY
or
INTELLIGENCE SUMMARY

(Erase heading not required.)

Army Form C.2118/56

Place	Date	Hour	Summary of Events and Information	Remarks and references to Appendices
La Forgue	1/1/17		Inspected the first line transport of 1/4, 1/6, 1/7 Inf Bde etc., was accompanied by officers from 91 Field Ordnance [?] Co.	6. D.T.4
"	2/1/17		Continued inspection of first line transport of 1st Division	6. D.T.4
			1/5 R.S.F. made etc.	
"	3/1/17		Continued my inspection of transport, visited 1/1 R.F.A. etc the artillery mobile units. In continuing inspection of transport & Rifle etc visited 1/M Div	6. D.T.4
			visits Artillery Units	6. D.T.4
"	4/1/17		Continued the inspection of 1M transport, commanding lecture 1/M Div	6. D.T.4
"	5/1/17		Concluded the inspection of transport work; Lieut. Brett, Lieutenant Inspector	6. D.T.4
"	6/1/17		Engaged [?] on departmental work	6. D.T.4
			Armourer visits the Div. Armourer Shop	
"	7/1/17		Submitted work to general, according to Davis Christie-sentto return to Base	6. D.T.4
			Rifles — range & inspects the clothing [?] return to Base	
"	8/1/17		Rifles — range & inspects the clothing/Armourer shops at 1M HQ Dps. [?] peak	6. D.T.4
			Arrangements made for starting an Armourers' shop	
"	9/1/17		Interview made with Div General for the purpose of obtaining some material for Armoured	6. D.T.4
			Visits Bethune from 1/1/17	
			Fortier S. Pol Pre	
"	10/1/17		Had a visit from 1/M a.a. + D 1/M.J. 1/M. Division who inspects "Shops". Arm shop + discussed several matter affecting the equipment of troops—etc. of efficiency	6. D.T.4

WAR DIARY
or
INTELLIGENCE SUMMARY
(Erase heading not required.)

Army Form C. 2118

Place	Date	Hour	Summary of Events and Information	Remarks and references to Appendices
La Fosse	11/1/17		Called at the Div. Workshops. The four battalions of the 167 Inf. Brigade	A. D. T.
"	12/1/17		Superintended the work of the Bgde.	A. D. T.
"	13/1/17		Assistant Inspector of Armourers visits Div. Wkshps.	W. D. T.
"	14/1/17		168th Brigade Armourers' Shop was visited by the Assistant Inspector of Armourers	W. D. T.
"	15/1/17		With Grading Officer sent to Div. from Ordnance & Engineers to the audition of N.C.Os from to Inf. machine gun Corps; subsequently to the sub areas of M.G. tractor stores belonging to Divisional Ammunition proceeded to the Salt Caves & Camp of the Division inspects M. Ordnance workshops.	A. D. T.
"	16/1/17		The J.O.B. & K.R.R. & Camp of the Division inspects M. Ordnance workshops	A. D. T.
"	17/1/17		Visits the I Co. Div. Train & interviews the Commanding officer. Also calls at the HQ Br of the 167, 168 & 169 Inf. Bgdes & confirms the unit's infantry workshops. These formations by an arrangement of the Div. Stop Ammunition Column throughout the day with experienced work	O. D. T.
	18/1/17		Occupied "	A. D. T.
	19/1/17		"	A. D. T.

WAR DIARY
or
INTELLIGENCE SUMMARY
(Erase heading not required.)

Army Form C. 211

Instructions regarding War Diaries and Intelligence Summaries are contained in F. S. Regs., Part II. and the Staff Manual respectively. Title Pages will be prepared in manuscript.

Place	Date	Hour	Summary of Events and Information	Remarks and references to Appendices
La Jofre	20/1/17		The Ambulant Inspector of Armoury (Lieut Lusette) visits the Div Shop	b. S74
"	21/1/17		Brig Gen Thornhill the day in attending to the administration of Ordnance Services with the Div: will not defend (report) from STI representation of October	b. S74
"	22/1/17		Departmental duties general supervision required in Workshop. Div Coy	b. S74
"	23/1/17		Attends administrative Conference at Div HQ Co to consider questions bearing on active operations	b. S74
"	24/1/17		Daily visits to the various administration with the Divison	b. S74
"	25/1/17		Attending General SM work of my Dept	b. S74
"	26/1/17		A.D.O.S. visiting Ordnance Dumps & workshops	b. S74
"	27/1/17		Supervising Ordnance administration general	b. S74
"	28/1/17		Was visited by A.D.O.S. XI Corps who interviewed some members of staff in connection with supplies furnished.	b. S74
"	29/1/17		Departmental work supervision attention throughout the day. Occupies with the routine work of Ordnance. The Inspector of Ordnance Machinery & a member of his staff a rang of Div occupies in inspecting work of Depot	b. S74
"	30/1/17		& members of his party attached a ramp of Div carrying out inspection of Depot	b. S74
"	31/1/17		articles details required the informant paid factory armoury work of Depot W.F. Robinson Lt. Col	b. S74

Capt & adj 2/5 56 Divsn

War Diary

DADOS

February 1917

WAR DIARY
or
INTELLIGENCE SUMMARY

Army Form C. 2118.

Place	Date	Hour	Summary of Events and Information	Remarks and references to Appendices
La Gorgue	1/2/19		The Divisional Commander accompanied by Lt A.A. & D.A.Q.M.G. inspected the Advanced stores & workshops belonging 57th Division	b. D.74
"	2/2/17	10am	Engaged on departmental work throughout the day	b. D.74
"	3/2/17		Lieut Lewis, A.D.O., arrived from 5th Div. recommenced his tour of inspection of the Shoemakers' Shops of this Div.	W. D74
"	4/2/17		Accompanied by Lieut Lewis (Boot expert) visited the Regimental Workshops of the 167 Inf Bde, & D.the 5 Cheshires (Pioneers) & H.Q. Gr 169 Inf Bde. Lt. D.the 167 Inf Bde. & D.the Lewis completed inspection of the regimental	b. D.74
"	5/2/17		Accompanied by Lieut Lewis inspection of 57th Division	b. D74
"	6/2/17		Lieut Lewis left for I Corps; engaged on departmental work	b. D74
"	7/2/17		Occupied throughout the day in administering the affairs of my dept E.	b. D74
"	8/2/17		Summary work inspected in Office & Gun workshops. Lieut D.B. Wilkinson made some kind of furnaces	c. D74
"	9/2/17		visited the Head Qrs of 167, 168 & 169th Inf Bdes	W. D74
"	10/2/17		Occupies throughout day with the routine work of my dept E.	b. D74
"	11/2/17			

Army Form C. 2118.

WAR DIARY
or
INTELLIGENCE SUMMARY
(Erase heading not required.)

Instructions regarding War Diaries and Intelligence Summaries are contained in F. S. Regs., Part II. and the Staff Manual respectively. Title Pages will be prepared in manuscript.

Place	Date	Hour	Summary of Events and Information	Remarks and references to Appendices
La Gorgue	12/2/17		Mr A.D.O.S. & XI Corps, accompanied by A.A. & XI Corps, visited workshops	6, DT#
"	13/2/17		Stopped at workshops the day	6, DT#
"	14/2/17		Days in Infantry journal, the work of my Office	6, DT# three workshops
"	15/2/17		Attended before at 1st Army HQ On by hind of hosts AA & AMG II Div on administrative arrangements, conducted by Divisional Repair	W DT#
"	16/2/17		Observing Practice. Arranged with Capt Upward Div. Salvage Officer, to assist in the Ypres during my absence on leave	W DT# 6 DT#
"	17/2/17		Took over from Col Stephenson. Inspected workshops stores. Routine work	work
"	18/2/17		Occupied in routine work all day	work
"	19/2/17		With DAQMG 36 Div inspected shops & stores. Usual routine work	work
"	20/2/17		Occupied in usual routine work	work
"	21/2/17		Usual routine duties occupied me all day	work
"	22/2/17		Attended lecture at 1st Army HQ by Brig Gen May	work

Army Form C. 2118.

WAR DIARY
or
INTELLIGENCE SUMMARY
(Erase heading not required.)

Instructions regarding War Diaries and Intelligence Summaries are contained in F. S. Regs., Part II. and the Staff Manual respectively. Title Pages will be prepared in manuscript.

Place	Date	Hour	Summary of Events and Information	Remarks and references to Appendices
La Gorgue	23/2/17		Supervision of shops and office and usual routine work	work
"	24/2/17		Rev to line to make local purchases	work
"	25/2/17		Usual routine work in stores & office ac	work
"	26/2/17		Inspected armoures lakes rootedless shops. Usual office work	work
"	27/2/17		Engaged in work in stores & office	work
"	28/2/17		Resumed duty after leave of absence was engaged in supervising work generally	G. J. H.

W. J. Hutchinson
Capt
BAOOS
56 Divn

2449 Wt. W14957/M90 750,000 1/16 J.B.C. & A. Forms/C.2118/12.

Headquarters,
56 Divn
Q Branch

D.A.D.O.S.
56th Divn
No. M2/27
Date. 2-4-17.

Herewith my "War Diary"
for the month of March 1917.
please.

W. D. Harhisin
Capt
DADOS
56 Divn

Army Form C. 2118.

Vol /4

WAR DIARY
or
INTELLIGENCE SUMMARY

(Erase heading not required.)

Instructions regarding War Diaries and Intelligence Summaries are contained in F. S. Regs., Part II. and the Staff Manual respectively. Title Pages will be prepared in manuscript.

Place	Date	Hour	Summary of Events and Information	Remarks and references to Appendices
La Jogue	1/3/1917		Arranged preliminaries preparatory to the removal of Div. HdQrs & Transport to Behavior Office & Stores	6, D74
"	2/3/17		Made additional arrangements necessitated by the move of Div H.Q Qrs	6, D74
"	3/3/17		Saw Dragons & 9 Div who will take over by Office & Stores & definitely informed them that he could take handover on 6 inst.	6, D74
"	4/4/17		Phone A/ material for workshop stores & accounts transferred to new area	6, D74
"	5/4/17		Continued transferring stores & works to Home	6, D74
"	6/4/17		Left La Jorgue with Div HdQrs for Wand	6, D74
Wand	7/4/17		At Wand & received instructions to proceed to Le Canny	6, D74
"	8/4/17		Transport Office & workshops to Le Canny. Div. HdQrs at	6, D74
Le Canny	9/4/17		Superintending Office & workshops across Div Hd Qrs at Le Canny.	6, D74
Le Canny	10/4/17		At Le Canny Storehouses. The day attending bomb practice. Res. 6, D74	6, D74
"	11/4/17		Received visit from A.D.D.S. HH Corps. My practice work for 4th day to occupied me probably on The day.	6, D74

Army Form C. 2118

WAR DIARY
or
INTELLIGENCE SUMMARY
(Erase heading not required.)

Instructions regarding War Diaries and Intelligence Summaries are contained in F.S. Regs., Part II. and the Staff Manual respectively. Title Pages will be prepared in manuscript.

Place	Date	Hour	Summary of Events and Information	Remarks and references to Appendices
Le Cauroy	12/3/17		Visits III Army Hrs; 184th workshops; apparent kitchen at Frevent market one bad puncture	6 DH
"	13/3/17		Visits A.D.O.S. VII Corps at Corps Hd Qrs; HEBUTS arms store	6 DH
"	14/3/17		For D.O. VII Corps. 12th pm Occupies in inspecting Gen 14½pm VII Corps M.T. dep. formed	6 DH
"	15/3/17		Went stores for M before Ypres; Runaway material apparent; visited by Gen rest Maxwell from Base	W. 8TH
"	16/3/17		Superintending the administration In depts; two visits by A.D.O.S. VIII Corps at Hd Qr S.D. Gen Gatacher at Ordnance store	6 DH
"	17/3/17		Went through Divn area visited at Souverneux; store there is an Ordnance group Gorry; also steppes at Souverneux 16:9 BDQ	6 STK
"	18/3/17		Div Hd Qrs move to Beaumetz; 1st Ordnance to Namen Lane from M present	6 8TH
"	19/3/17		Div Hd Qrs move to Beaumetz; 1st Gd D.V.S + Ordnance store + workshop remain for M present at Le Cauroy	6 DH

Army Form C. 2118

WAR DIARY
or
INTELLIGENCE SUMMARY
(Erase heading not required.)

Instructions regarding War Diaries and Intelligence Summaries are contained in F. S. Regs., Part II. and the Staff Manual respectively. Title Pages will be prepared in manuscript.

Place	Date	Hour	Summary of Events and Information	Remarks and references to Appendices
Le Cauroy	20/3/17		Superintending work by personnel during the day.	S.74
Le Cauroy	21/3/17		Unit standing. Gen. inspected "Dump". Starting at present for storing supplies Shot. Also horses came up & rifles & steel helmets from O.O. Army Troops No 2, 7 remount.	W. S.74
"	22/3/17		Commenced transferring Brimar stores to Div H.Q. or at Beaumetz le Loges	W. S.74
Beaumetz	23/3/17		Removed office, dump, workshop, personnel to Beaumetz	W. S.74
"	24/3/17		Superintending the arrangement of office, workshop at new H.Qrs	S.74
"	25/3/17		Visits to the M van Div and transport workshops shore	S.74
"	26/3/17		Superintending Brimar work in Div	S.74
"	27/3/17		Went to Amiens to receive returned engine regime by Gr	W. S.74
"	28/3/17		Motor down by Capt VII Corps H Red GIV.G 55 Gr	S.74
"	29/3/17		Attended conference at M. Office of Corps VII C.E/S	S.74
"	30/3/17		Superintending work by Div Dep & fredees	W. S.74
"	31/3/17		Visits to Field transp wkshp return of tools SM Bond S.Horkiw tr Div tr	W. S.74

Captain O.C.

Headquarters
56 Divn.

> D.A.D.O.S.,
> 56th DIVISION,
> No. M2/2a
> Date. 1-5-17

Herewith please find my
War Diary for the month of April
1917.

C. D. Harbinson
Capt
D.A.D.O.S
56 Divn

WAR DIARY or INTELLIGENCE SUMMARY

Army Form C. 2118

(Erase heading not required.)

Instructions regarding War Diaries and Intelligence Summaries are contained in F.S. Regs., Part II. and the Staff Manual respectively. Title Pages will be prepared in manuscript.

Place	Date	Hour	Summary of Events and Information	Remarks and references to Appendices
Beaumetz les Loges	1/4/17		Posts Several miles but damp at present & intent to open attacks for return to troops at Bn H.Q.	
"	2/4/17		Pershine took G.H.Q Staff round ex Rumsbout the br	
"	3/4/17		Went to Dornburg & Lt. Inglis & fac Ohuckery instead for Majr the made a Bn. Comply of Ohuckery	
"	4/4/17		Ruthey details arranging to view Ohuckery Ohurn	
"	5/4/17		Northern	
"	6/4/17		Superintending return took Bourne B.	
"	7/4/17		Superintended work arrangements grouping the Bn	
"	8/4/17		Buses attaching to movements & details necessitated by information for military Matters	
"	9/4/17		Most ley attached p B.N. never rather the more up movements.	
"	9/4/17		Spent day in Bn office	
"	9/4/17		States III Army from Park & Henry Hubel Instructions—Lts at Present fulls sufficient of Phleering spear park for forces	
"	10/4/17		Occupies with getting as of Release administration Salary te to W.D.W.	

WAR DIARY or INTELLIGENCE SUMMARY

Army Form C. 2118

Place	Date	Hour	Summary of Events and Information	Remarks and references to Appendices
Beaumetz les loges	11/4/17		Two visits a.m. "Dumps" b, A, B, C, V, VII Corps	6/S.W.
"	12/4/17		Commenced returns. Visits Warlincourt & R. Bange	5 S.W.
"	13/4/17		Visits III Army Gen Park. Prevented conversion with stores on demand for Divs; also calls at Div Baths, Hurlercourt + remains clothing ready for return.	6 S.W.
"	14/4/17		Base. Occupies Pomphart by orders I.E. with H.Q. (routine work of my Staff)	5.9 S.W.
"	15/4/17		Visits advanced Div HQ Div, also Supreme arts at Achicourt for Infantry advanced Schemes Dumps.	4 S.W.
"	16/4/17		Visits railhead at Arras + infantry/cavalry operations at Tilloy. advanced dump at Achicourt	6 S.W.
"	17/4/17		Spent by at advanced dumps + advanced HQ Div	15 S.W.
"	18/4/17		Visits A.D.S., VII Corps Rehearsed arrangements to Infantry to leave Corps area.	
"	19/4/17		Visits A.D.S. XVIII Corps + made front tents to for refitting & rein inward it moves into back area	W.D.A.
"	20/4/17		Commenced removing stores from advanced Div Dump at Achicourt.	6 S.W.

WAR DIARY
or
INTELLIGENCE SUMMARY

(Erase heading not required.)

Army Form C. 2118

Instructions regarding War Diaries and Intelligence Summaries are contained in F.S. Regs., Part II. and the Staff Manual respectively. Title Pages will be prepared in manuscript.

Place	Date	Hour	Summary of Events and Information	Remarks and references to Appendices
Beaumetz	21/4/17		Portion of stores sent to new Bgd. Dumps at Sorastre in new Div. area.	65 Bty.
"	22/4/17		Completed removal of stores & workshops to Sorastre	65 Bty.
Sorastre	23/4/17		Commenced the process of refitting the Div.	65 Bty.
"	24/4/17		Continues the reissue of stores to & refitting of Div. units.	65 Bty.
"	25/4/17		Received orders from Div. to move Dumps away to change of area. Arrangements to move Dumps, Workshops to move to Beaumetz. Head & Sty of Dumps, workshops re-installed at Beaumetz.	65 Bty.
"	26/4/17			65 Bty. b. 5th
"	27/4/17		Visits 3rd Army Gun Park in connection with workshops for Div. Also made line for parts for Div. at Amiens. Superintends the issue of limber drury 14 day remount Div.	65 Bty.
"	28/4/17		Hd. Qrs with Inf.	O.B. 74
Arras	29/4/17		Removes Ordnance Dumps, Workshops to Arras, corps	65 Bty.
"	30/4/17		Attends a conference at all Officers of action VII Corps	65 Bty.

b. J. Harbinson
Capt.
N & L of Dir

Headquarters
56 Division.

Herewith Monthly War Diary
for May 1917 from DADOS

Rutledge
for DADOS
56 Divn.

1/6/17

WAR DIARY
or
INTELLIGENCE SUMMARY

(Erase heading not required.)

Army Form C. 2118.

WO 95/56?
JJ/16

Instructions regarding War Diaries and Intelligence Summaries are contained in F.S. Regs., Part II. and the Staff Manual respectively. Title Pages will be prepared in manuscript.

Place	Date	Hour	Summary of Events and Information	Remarks and references to Appendices
Arras	1/5/17		Wrote to III Army for report in regard to collection of stores; also III Army Heavy Artil workshops for a similar purpose	
"	2/5/17		D.D.O.S. III Army paid a visit to my First workshops	
"	3/5/17		With Gardiner (my N/S for workshops) group at Frevent. Learned between this important places there by noon — the statement & returned to Group 78	
"	4/5/17		Inspecting the work of my Staff Sergeant Armourer	
"	5/5/17		Arryt. to armourers my workshop & instructing the Ordnance armr. & M.Gunn M.Gunn.	
"	6/5/17		Creates spare parts for the III Corps for Park Frevent	
"	7/5/17		Made some small local purchases at St. Pol	
"	8/5/17		Ordnance workshop 1 Day with tt routine duties	
"	9/5/17		Received a visit from D.A.D.O.S. III Army; also from A.D.O.S. VI Corps W.S.H	
"	10/5/17		Went to G.H.Q. Pol & Boulogne Purchased articles of Armourers that were urgently needed by Div.	

Army Form C. 2118.

WAR DIARY
or
INTELLIGENCE SUMMARY
(Erase heading not required.)

Instructions regarding War Diaries and Intelligence Summaries are contained in F. S. Regs., Part II. and the Staff Manual respectively. Title Pages will be prepared in manuscript.

Place	Date	Hour	Summary of Events and Information	Remarks and references to Appendices
Arras	11/5/17		Proc. S.C. in attending S.L. routine work. P.Z. Paris Departmental work in Division people	63ff
"	12/5/17		Departmental work in Division people. Telephone to say trip to GO Dr. SL Sir Ashley to telegraph call upon AOMS	63ff
"	13/5/17		VI Corps	63ff
"	14/5/17		Attends conference at H. Office of A.D.M.S. VII Corps re contracts	63ff, 159ff
"	15/5/17		Supervising Ordnance armaments	
"	16/5/17		See Head D.D.S. Visits to J.A.D.O.S., 37 R. Div. etc, noted 25 trumps & water to keep at A.D.M.S. 37 Div. etc. 37 to P.O. Lecks P.S. 37.	63ff
"	17/5/17		Staff orders taken one by him Dep. D.D.S. Dunum visits Sapters Kit Dumps at Perant & Mt. St. Eloy D.D.T. Dunum inspecting out Bedrine & state hosp & reports	374
				63ff
"	18/5/17		Nine Calls upon A.D.M.S. VI Corps re telegraph sent to Danville & for a confm. inspect (left has been furlough) in accordance with full instruction received	63ff
	19/5/17		Duties during today until the routine work of my dept.	63ff

WAR DIARY or INTELLIGENCE SUMMARY

Army Form C. 2118.

Place	Date	Hour	Summary of Events and Information	Remarks and references to Appendices
Arras Habarcq	20/5/17		Made arrangements to transfer Dump, Workshops etc to Habarcq	A.S.74
Habarcq	21/5/17		Established Dump workshops at Habarcq in accordance with Divisional Commands	A.S.74 A.S.74
"	22/5/17		Received day arrangement workshops etc at Habarcq	A.S.74
"	23/5/17		Visited VII Corps rear A.D.O.S. for return of stores during his absence on leave	A.S.74
"	24/5/17		Staff day superintending the work in shops in work shops	A.S.74
"	25/5/17		VII Corps diapered Duette helpers A.D.O.S. Lieut & Capt 2 guides.g.f.g. Visited Hd Qr VII Corps & left & hospital also went and visited shell connection with Armonin Depot future 16 Inf Bn. Superintended the administration of 4 Infty units E to HV Div. M og.	A.S.74 A.S.74
"	26/5/17			A.S.74
"	27/5/17		Received instructions for 3 Army Horses Dept on 19 Pooh to take on temporary the duties of A.D.O.S.	A.S.74 A.S.74
"	28/5/17		Duties of Dadas handed over temporarily to Lieut Jw. Burbidge AOD	

Army Form C. 2118.

WAR DIARY
or
INTELLIGENCE SUMMARY.
(Erase heading not required.)

Place	Date	Hour	Summary of Events and Information	Remarks and references to Appendices
Murray	29/5/17		Regimental Routine	J. Brophy Lt [?]
"	30/5/17		do	
"	31/5/17		do	

J. Rutherford
Major
f. [?] Bn 26 Div.

WAR DIARY
or
INTELLIGENCE SUMMARY.
(Erase heading not required.)

Army Form C. 2118.

DA555 56B
1917

Place	Date	Hour	Summary of Events and Information	Remarks and references to Appendices
Mahony	June 1		Departmental Routine	
"	2		Visited Amiens for local purchases	
"	3		Departmental Routine	
"	4		do.	
"	5		do.	
"	6		Preparations for removal of dump	
"	7		Visited proposed new dump	
"	8		Visited HQrs by lorries, making arrangements for taking over attached units	
"	9		Departmental Routine	
"	10		Placed in charge of moving stores to new dump	
"	11			
Achcheux	12		New dump opened	

Army Form C. 2118.

WAR DIARY
or
INTELLIGENCE SUMMARY.
(Erase heading not required.)

Instructions regarding War Diaries and Intelligence Summaries are contained in F.S. Regs., Part II. and the Staff Manual respectively. Title pages will be prepared in manuscript.

Place	Date	Hour	Summary of Events and Information	Remarks and references to Appendices
Advanct	June 13		Visited "I Corps" Salvage Dump, Depot 18th & 21st Divisions	JM.D
"	" 14		Visited Tournai, St Pol, Ambleteuse for Local Purchases	JM.D
"	" 15		Amiens for Local purchases	JM.D
"	" 16		Departmental routine	JM.D
"	" 17		Visited Matthews	JM.D
"	" 18		Departmental routine	JM.D
"	" 19		VI Corps Advance Conference	JM.D
"	" 20		Local Purchases at Tournai	JM.D
"	" 21		Departmental Duties	JM.D
"	" 22		Visited Local A.Stations in search of Employer Circulars etc	JM.D
"	" 23		Depots 61st & 33 Division	JM.D
"	" 24		Departmental routine A.O.S. VI Corps Visited dumps	Anderson
"	" 25		Visited railhead as Army Headquarters	JA
"	" 26		Departmental duties	JA

Army Form C. 2118.

WAR DIARY
or
INTELLIGENCE SUMMARY.
(Erase heading not required.)

Instructions regarding War Diaries and Intelligence Summaries are contained in F. S. Regs., Part II. and the Staff Manual respectively. Title pages will be prepared in manuscript.

Place	Date	Hour	Summary of Events and Information	Remarks and references to Appendices
Achicourt	1917 June 27		Departmental duties	ya
"	" 28		ADOS VI Corps visited store	ya
"	" 29		Departmental duties	ya
"	" 30		Departmental duties	ya

Henderson Lt Col
for ADOS

Army Form C. 2118.

WAR DIARY
or
INTELLIGENCE SUMMARY.
(Erase heading not required.)

Instructions regarding War Diaries and Intelligence Summaries are contained in F. S. Regs., Part II. and the Staff Manual respectively. Title pages will be prepared in manuscript.

Place	Date 1918	Hour	Summary of Events and Information	Remarks and references to Appendices
Achicourt	July 1		Departmental duties arranged for transfer of shops & stores to Le Cauroy.	
"	" 2		Moved shops and Reserves to Le Cauroy	
"	" 3		Completed move of Stores and detachment	
Le Cauroy	" 4		Departmental duties	
"	" 5		Visited Kitchen Corps Headquarters	
"	" 6		Departmental routine	
"	" 7		Inspected depôt Battalion stores	
"	" 8		Visited 167 Bde Stores	
"	" 9		do 168 " "	
"	" 10		do 169 " "	
"	" 11		Departmental duties	
"	" 12		Visited Haulliers for local purchases	
"	" 13		Usual routine	
"	" 14		Visited Forest for local purchases	

Army Form C. 2118.

D.A.D.O.S.
56th DIVISION.

WAR DIARY
or
INTELLIGENCE SUMMARY.
(Erase heading not required.)

Instructions regarding War Diaries and Intelligence Summaries are contained in F.S. Regs., Part II. and the Staff Manual respectively. Title pages will be prepared in manuscript.

Place	Date	Hour	Summary of Events and Information	Remarks and references to Appendices
St Leonard	July 15		Visited Railhead to make arrangements for moving	
"	" 16		Inspected Dispro Kit Dump. Took steps reference to Ordnance store	
"	" 17		Departmental routine	
"	" 18		Made arrangements for extra clothing etc.	
"	" 19		Departmental duties	
"	" 20		Visited Corps - Railhead	
"	" 21		Departmental routine	
"	" 22		Made arrangements for moving to Eperles tomorrow	
"	" 23		Moved to Eperlecques taking over from 11th Division transport	
EPERLECQUES	" 24		Visited by ADOS I Corps	
do	" 25		Departmental duties	
do	" 26		Visited Gun Park Base	
do	" 27		Inspected various units stores	

Army Form C. 2118

WAR DIARY
or
INTELLIGENCE SUMMARY.
(Erase heading not required.)

D.A.D.O.S.
59th DIVISION.

Place	Date	Hour	Summary of Events and Information	Remarks and references to Appendices
FONTAINE EPERLECQUES	29 July 1917		Drew stores from Sun Park, Bolounanville. Made enquiries at Calais for missing trucks containing Ordnance.	
do	30		Departmental routine	
do	31		Inspected various units' workshops	

Jn Dunkley
Lieut
59th Div

Army Form C. 2

WAR DIARY
or
INTELLIGENCE SUMMARY.
(Erase heading not required.)

D.A.D.O.S.
58th DIVISION.

Place	Date 1917	Hour	Summary of Events and Information	Remarks and references to Appendices
ESQUEDECQ EPERLECQUES	Aug 1		Departmental duties	
"	" 2		Visited ADOS I Corps	
"	" 3		Checked indents with D.A.D.O.S. Army Base Park	
"	" 4		Made arrangements for transfer of store to Reninghelst	
"	" 5		Moving to Reninghelst	
Reninghelst	" 6		" " "	
"	" 7		Visited ADOS II Corps	
"	" 8		Departmental duties	
"	" 9		Visited to Calais for urgent stores	
"	" 10		Visited Corps Salvage Dumps	
"	" 11		Inspected Divl Laundry	
"	" 12		Departmental duties to it Divl Arty attached	
"	" 13		Obtained urgent stores from Calais Base	

Army Form C. 2118.

WAR DIARY
or
INTELLIGENCE SUMMARY.
(Erase heading not required.)

Instructions regarding War Diaries and Intelligence Summaries are contained in F. S. Regs., Part II. and the Staff Manual respectively. Title pages will be prepared in manuscript.

D.A.D.O.S.,
50TH DIVISION.

Place	Date	Hour	Summary of Events and Information	Remarks and references to Appendices
Remy pdt	1917 Aug 14		Road duckboard. Advance store removed at R'klair	
do	" 15		Visited Divisional Corps Salvage Dump	
do	" 16		Visited Corps Dressing Station & Cl. Station	
do	" 17		Departmental Routine	
do	" 18		Visited Railhead	
do	" 19		Visited 150 Bde. dump	
do	" 20		do 149 "	
do	" 21		do 67 "	
do	" 22		Departmental routine	
do	" 23		Visited dump 23rd Division	
do	set		Took over store of August 23rd div. at Eperlecques	
do	" 25		Visited ADOS V Corps	
Eperlecques	" 26		Cessations London 23rd Divison	
	" 27		ADOS XVIII Corps re urgent business	

Army Form C. 2118.
56th DIVISION

WAR DIARY
or
INTELLIGENCE SUMMARY.
(Erase heading not required.)

Place	Date	Hour	Summary of Events and Information	Remarks and references to Appendices
Monchique	Aug 1917 28		Routine work & inspn. Rehearsals & Co. Antions	B.S.
"	" 29		Preparations for removal to new area	B.S.
"	30		Moved to Frévent	B.S.
Frévent	" 31		Departmental Routine	B.S.

J.W. Rutledge
Lieut
Adjut 56 Divn.

WAR DIARY
or
INTELLIGENCE SUMMARY.
(Erase heading not required.)

Army Form C. 2118.

D.A.D.O.S., 56th DIVISION.

No. ....
Date ....

Instructions regarding War Diaries and Intelligence Summaries are contained in F. S. Regs., Part II. and the Staff Manual respectively. Title pages will be prepared in manuscript.

Place	Date	Hour	Summary of Events and Information	Remarks and references to Appendices
Premesques	1917 Sept 1		Visited ADOS IV Corps, Northern Workshops, Bapaume	
"	" 2		Departmental Routine	
"	" 3		do	
"	" 4		Divl Artillery repaired Division	
"	" 5		Visited Amiens for event purchasing	
"	" 6		Departmental Routine	
"	" 7		Northern Bapaume	
"	" 8		Visited ADOS IV Corps Conf, ADOS Northern	
"	" 9		Departmental Routine	
"	" 10		Visited Gun Park & My Mobile Workshop	
"	" 11		Brigade conference at HQ RHA HQ	
"	" 12		Inspection 166 Bde units stores	

Army Form C. 2118

WAR DIARY
or
INTELLIGENCE SUMMARY.

(Erase heading not required.)

D.A.D.O.S.
50th DIVISION

Instructions regarding War Diaries and Intelligence Summaries are contained in F. S. Regs., Part II. and the Staff Manual respectively. Title pages will be prepared in manuscript.

Place	Date	Hour	Summary of Events and Information	Remarks and references to Appendices
Fremicourt	Sept 13		Departmental Routine	
"	14		Inspected 67 Bde auto store	
"	15		Local purchase at Amiens	
"	16		Departmental Routine	
"	17		Visited ADOS IV Corps	
"	18		Inspection of blankets received from Paris at 5th Div MGR	
"	19		Div Soffices inspected by ADOS IV Corps	
"	20		Departmental Routine	
"	21		Local purchase at Corbie, Amiens, St Pol	
"	22		Inspected Q.M. stores of 168 Bde	
"	23		" " " " 169 Bde	
"	24		Departmental Routine	
"	25		do	

Army Form C. 2118

WAR DIARY
or
INTELLIGENCE SUMMARY.

(Erase heading not required.)

Instructions regarding War Diaries and Intelligence Summaries are contained in F. S. Regs., Part II. and the Staff Manual respectively. Title pages will be prepared in manuscript.

D.A.D.S.S.
50th DIVISION.

Place	Date	Hour	Summary of Events and Information	Remarks and references to Appendices
Frévent	1917 Sept 26		Departmental Routine	
"	27		Local Purchase of Ammo at Albert	
"	28		Visited Gun Park Ruitz [?]	
"	29		Inspected 158 Bde. ammn stores	
"	30		Departmental Routine	

J. Mackay
Major
D.A.D.S.S.

Army Form C. 2118

WAR DIARY
or
INTELLIGENCE SUMMARY.

(Erase heading not required.)

D.A.D.O.S.
56th DIVISION.

Instructions regarding War Diaries and Intelligence Summaries are contained in F. S. Regs., Part II. and the Staff Manual respectively. Title pages will be prepared in manuscript.

Place	Date	Hour	Summary of Events and Information	Remarks and references to Appendices
Fremicourt	1917 October 1		Store workshops inspected by A.D.O.S.	
"	" 2		Departmental routine	
"	" 3		Store & workshops inspected by D.D.O.S. Third Army	
"	" 4		Local purchase of horses	
"	" 5		Departmental routine	
"	" 6		Visited Gun Park, Bullhurst & Corps Headquarters	
"	" 7		Attended Artillery Conference	
"	" 8		Local purchasing in Albert & Amiens	
"	" 9		Departmental duties	
"	" 10		Departmental duties. Visited by A.D.O.S	
"	" 11		Departmental Routine	
"	" 12		Departmental Routine	
"	" 13		Departmental Routine	
"	" 14		Departmental Routine	

Army Form C. 2118

WAR DIARY
or
INTELLIGENCE SUMMARY.
(Erase heading not required.)

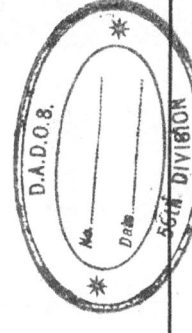

56th DIVISION

Place	Date	Hour	Summary of Events and Information	Remarks and references to Appendices
Frémicourt	Dec 1917	15	Departmental duties	
"	"	16	Departmental duties	
"	"	17	Departmental duties	
"	"	18	Road purchases at Amiens	
"	"	19	Departmental duties	
"	"	20	First consignment of winter clothing arrived	
"	"	21	Major-General Bloxham, DSO Army and his staff visited store	
"	"	22	Departmental duties	
"	"	23	Departmental duties	
"	"	24	Local purchases at Amiens	
"	"	25	Visited road to Albert	
"	"	26	Departmental duties	
"	"	27	Visited Railhead	
"	"	28	Visited Gun Park	
"	"	29	Departmental duties	
"	"	30		
"	"	31	Visited 168 Bde O.M. Stores	

Army Form C. 2118.

WAR DIARY
or
INTELLIGENCE SUMMARY.
(Erase heading not required.)

D.A.D.O.S.,
56th DIVISION.

Place	Date	Hour	Summary of Events and Information	Remarks and references to Appendices
Doingheast	Nov 17	1	Local purchase at Amiens. Visited DADS Third Army	Duty
		2	Stores inspected by AA & QMG	"
		3	Visited Inspection Ordnance Dutio	"
		4	Departmental duties	"
		5	Front Line tour. Visited Havre	"
		6	Stores received by DADS Third Army	"
		7	do do from IV Corps	"
		8	Departmental duties	"
		9	do	"
		10	Stores inspected by DADOS	"
		11	Conference in Amiens	"
		12	Departmental duties	"
		13	Visited Railhead	"
		14	Visited Army Field Workshops & also last workshop	"
		15	Conference	"

Army Form C. 2118.

WAR DIARY
or
INTELLIGENCE SUMMARY.
(Erase heading not required.)

D.A.D.O.S, 56th DIVISION.

No. ....
Date ....

Instructions regarding War Diaries and Intelligence Summaries are contained in F.S. Regs., Part II. and the Staff Manual respectively. Title pages will be prepared in manuscript.

Place	Date	Hour	Summary of Events and Information	Remarks and references to Appendices
Inchiville	Nov. 16		Issued about 7 tops	
"	17		Heavy rain. Horses San Pol	
"	18		Evacuated sick	
"	19			
"	20		Lent lorries in Review detail	
"	21		Shalented lorries	
"	22		Inspected 1/1 Sec. mf. chan	
"	23		Inspection made by Genl	
"	24		Regimental Review	
"	25		Horses drawn in for field holdings	
"	26		do	workshop
"	27		Regimental holdings	
"	28		Horses sent to bigs	
"	29		Regimental Review	
"	30		Local purchase lumber	

Murphy
Capt.
A.D.O.S. 56th Div.

Army Form C. 2118.

WAR DIARY
or
INTELLIGENCE SUMMARY.

(Erase heading not required.)

D.A.D.O.S., 56th DIVISION.

Instructions regarding War Diaries and Intelligence Summaries are contained in F.S. Regs., Part II. and the Staff Manual respectively. Title pages will be prepared in manuscript.

Place	Date	Hour	Summary of Events and Information	Remarks and references to Appendices
	November			
Trenaud	1		Preparations for moving	Published
"	2		Handing over to 51st Division	do
Frévex	3		On the move	do
"	4		Handing over to Canada Division	do
St Catherine Arras	5		Taking over from 31st Division	do
"	6		Operational Routine	do
"	7		Visited ADOS VIII Corps	do
"	8		Departmental Routine	do
"	9		" "	do
"	10		Lieut Purchase at Ordnance School visited me & left	do
"	11		Departmental Routine	do
"	12		" "	do
"	13		Inspected 1/5 Cheshires transport	do

Army Form C. 2118.

D.A.D.O.S.,
56th DIVISION.
No............
Date............

WAR DIARY
or
INTELLIGENCE SUMMARY.
(Erase heading not required.)

Place	Date	Hour	Summary of Events and Information	Remarks and references to Appendices
St Catherines	Sept	14	Units inspected at Camp	
Camp		15	Unit inspected by CRA XIII Corps. Equip Practice in Camp.	
		16	Reps transport inspected	
		17	Visited Workshops, 115 Machine & SP A AW	
		18	Superintended handing over log Qu.	
		19	Inspected clothing stores. Bath houses	
		20	" " " to battling schools	
		21	Visited DADSV 51 Divn re battling schools	
		22	Rtd returned Leuvens	
		23	Ditto	
		24	Made arrangements re stores porcelain — Ferme Richland	
		25	Visited ADOS XIII Corps, Gun Park & DADOS 33 Div	
		26	Proceeded to IV Ord Depot for ammunition lorries	

Army Form C. 2118.

WAR DIARY
or
INTELLIGENCE SUMMARY.
(Erase heading not required.)

D.A.D.O.S.,
56th DIVISION.

Place	Date	Hour	Summary of Events and Information	Remarks and references to Appendices
St Catherine Arras	Dec	27	Tour of inspection in front area to important dumps N. of Arras	M Richards
"	"	28	Departmental duties	"
"	"	29	Departmental routine	"
"	"	30	Stores & shops inspected by D.A. and Q.M.G.	"
"	"	31	Departmental routine	"

M Richards
Major
DADOS 56 Div

Army Form C. 2118.

WAR DIARY
or
INTELLIGENCE SUMMARY.
(Erase heading not required.)

D.A.D.O.S.,
56th DIVISION.

Instructions regarding War Diaries and Intelligence Summaries are contained in F. S. Regs., Part II. and the Staff Manual respectively. Title pages will be prepared in manuscript.

Place	Date	Hour	Summary of Events and Information	Remarks and references to Appendices
St Catherine	Jan 1918	1st	Departmental Routine	
Arras	"	2nd	Departmental Routine	
"	"	3rd	Visited Ivergues for selection of new billets	
"	"	4th	Departmental Routine	
"	"	5th	Visited A.D.O.S. 1st Corps re Departmental Duties	
"	"	6th	Departmental Routine	
"	"	7th	Departmental Routine	
"	"	8th	Moved stores from St Catherine to Ivergues	
Ivergues	"	9th	Departmental Duties	
"	"	10th	D.A.D.O.S. returned from Ammunition Course at No. 1 Ordnance Depot	
"	"	11th	Departmental Routine	
"	"	12th	Inspected 1/16 toy Field by A.D. Transport	
"	"	13th	Local Purchase in Arras	
"	"	14th	Visited H.Qrs 167 Bde	
"	"	15th	Inspected 8th M.G.s transport & stores	
"	"	16th	Visited A.O.D. XIII Corps	
"	"	17th	Departmental Routine	

Army Form C. 2118.

D.A.D.O.S.
56th DIVISION.

WAR DIARY
or
INTELLIGENCE SUMMARY.
(Erase heading not required.)

Instructions regarding War Diaries and Intelligence Summaries are contained in F. S. Regs., Part II. and the Staff Manual respectively. Title pages will be prepared in manuscript.

Place	Date 1918	Hour	Summary of Events and Information	Remarks and references to Appendices
Senegues	Jan 18		D.A.D.O.S left for leave to England - Departmental Duties	
"	" 19		Shops & Stores inspected by A.D.G.S & D.A.Q.M.G	
"	" 20		Visited by Staff Captain R.A - Departmental Duties	
"	" 21		Departmental Duties	
"	" 22		Visited by D.A.D.M.G - Departmental Duties	
"	" 23		Departmental routine	
"	" 24		Visited by D.A.Q.M.G - Departmental Duties	
"	" 25		Local Purchase in Etaires	
"	" 26		Visited A.D.O.S - Departmental Duties	
"	" 27		Visited by D.A.Q.M.G - Departmental Duties	
"	" 28		Departmental Duties, visited by D.A.D.M.G	
"	" 29		Taking in Stores from Disbanded Units in 3rd & 4th & 13 London Regts	
"	" 30		Visited by A.D.O.S - Taking in of stores from Disbanded Units completed	
"	" 31		Departmental routine - visited A.O.D and Stores inspected by D.A.Q.M.G	
"	Feb 1		Departmental routine visited by Staff Captain R.A	
"	" 2		Inspected of Guest House from Battalions to Base	
"	" 3		Visited App 55 by office - Departmental routine	

Army Form C. 2118.

WAR DIARY
—or—
INTELLIGENCE SUMMARY.
(Erase heading not required.)

Instructions regarding War Diaries and Intelligence Summaries are contained in F. S. Regs., Part II. and the Staff Manual respectively. Title pages will be prepared in manuscript.

D.A.D.O.S.
56th DIVISION.
No. ....
Date ....

Place	Date 1918	Hour	Summary of Events and Information	Remarks and references to Appendices
Arques	Feb 1st		Departmental Routine – visited by Staff Captain RA	
"	" 2nd		Despatched all special stores from Ordnance Battalion to Corps	
"	" 3rd		Visited DADOS 53 DIV HQ at Hopoutre – Departmental Routine	
"	" 4th		Departmental Routine – visited Lea Dept at Quay + Pros Stores Trakes	
"	" 5th		Departmental Routine – visited by DADMS – Stables inspected	
"	6		Inspection of Artillery Vehicles	
"	7		Local Purchase Board	
"	8		Corps Conference	
"	9		Departmental Routine	
"	10		Preparations for moving	
"	11		Moved Office & stores	
"	12		Inspected 169 Bde QM stores	
St Antoine Arm	13		Visited Railhead Mobile Workshop. Local Purchase on Amiens	
"	14		Departmental Routine	
"	15		Inspection of 168 Bde QM Stores	
"	16		Departmental Routine	

Army Form C. 2118.

WAR DIARY
or
INTELLIGENCE SUMMARY.
(Erase heading not required.)

D.A.D.O.S.
54th DIVISION.

Place	Date	Hour	Summary of Events and Information	Remarks and references to Appendices
St Catherines Area	Feb 1918	17	Inspection by A.D.M.S. First Army, accompanied by A.D.O.S. VIII Corps	
"		18	Inspection of Salvage Dump	
"		19	Routine	
"		20	Routine	
"		21	Reconnaissance — Forward Artillery	
"		22	Inspected Salvaged ammunition	
"		23	Visited Ruitz End	
"		24	Routine	
"		25	Routine	
"		26	Inspection of A.R.D. by D.D.C.	
"		27	Local Purchase. Wooden iron cups	
"		28	Visited O.P.D. Corps hour Salvage Dump & A.R.P.	

Army Form C. 2118.

D.A.D.O.S.,
56th DIVISION.
No. ....
Date ....

WAR DIARY
or
INTELLIGENCE SUMMARY.
(Erase heading not required.)

Instructions regarding War Diaries and Intelligence Summaries are contained in F. S. Regs., Part II. and the Staff Manual respectively. Title pages will be prepared in manuscript.

Place	Date	Hour	Summary of Events and Information	Remarks and references to Appendices
St Catherine	1918			
Arras	March 1		Visited Railhead. Inspected transport	
"	2		Inspect MG Battalion Transport	
"	3		Instructional visit to the Army Salvage Dump	
"	4		Local purchase in Amiens. Visited A.D.O.S. VIII Corps	
"	5		Local purchase in Arras. Visited Ordnance Rly Rd	
"	6		Routine	
"	7		Routine	
"	8		Visited about 37 Division	
"	9		Visited Depot & Divisions	
"	10		Routine	
"	11		Visited our VIII Corps. Local purchase in Arras	
"	12		Routine. Visited Railhead	
"	13		Inspection of 280 Coy R.F.A. Wagon Line	

(A7092). Wt. W12839/M1293. 75,000. 1/17. D. D. & L., Ltd. Forms/C.2118/14.

Army Form C. 2118.

D.A.D.O.S.
56th DIVISION.

WAR DIARY
or
INTELLIGENCE SUMMARY.
(Erase heading not required.)

Instructions regarding War Diaries and Intelligence Summaries are contained in F. S. Regs., Part II. and the Staff Manual respectively. Title pages will be prepared in manuscript.

Place	Date	Hour	Summary of Events and Information	Remarks and references to Appendices
St Valery	14		Inspection of 1st Rde R.F.A. Major Rose. Departmental duties	
"	15		Reading	
"	16		Visited by D.A.D.O.S. Departmental Duties	
"	17		Visited by Inspector of Armourers. Departmental Duties	
"	18		Departmental duties	
"	19		Visited by D.A.D.O.S. & Shops inspected. Departmental duties	
"	20		Departmental Duties	
"	21		Inspected equipment of 2/3 Field Ambulance	
"	22		Departmental Duties. Visited Railhead	
"	23		Visited A.D.O.S. Departmental Duties	
"	24		Moved G.H.Q. to Bray	
Bray	25		Moved Stores to Bray. Departmental Duties	
"	26		Lecture	
"	27		Visited Railhead Crow.	
"	28		Preparations for moving to Agnuis	

Army Form C. 2118.

WAR DIARY
or
INTELLIGENCE SUMMARY.

(Erase heading not required.)

D.A.D.O.S.
56th DIVISION.

Instructions regarding War Diaries and Intelligence
Summaries are contained in F. S. Regs., Part II.
and the Staff Manual respectively. Title pages
will be prepared in manuscript.

Place	Date	Hour	Summary of Events and Information	Remarks and references to Appendices
France	Mar.	29	Visited 2/6 & 8th Bgde	
		30	Rouen	
		31	Visited gun park & 167 & 168 light Rail Hd	

Army Form C.2118.

"WAR" DIARY
or
INTELLIGENCE SUMMARY.
(Erase heading not required.)

D.A.D.O.S.
56th DIVISION.

Instructions regarding War Diaries and Intelligence Summaries are contained in F.S. Regs., Part II. and the Staff Manual respectively. Title pages will be prepared in manuscript.

Place	Date	Hour	Summary of Events and Information	Remarks and references to Appendices
Agnez	Apl	1	Routine	
		2	Tractor finished	
		3	Routine	
		4	Tested Gun Park & by 1st Army Insp.	
		5	Tested 1/5 & 1/7 Insp. Regt. into Stores	
		6	Sending in sub for trench mortars	
		7	Preparing for move to Monchiet	
Monchiet		8	Moved dump to Monchiet	
		9	Writes away VIII Corps A.O.	
		10	Inspected 53 ams Waggon	
		11	Routine	
		12	Visited GHQ & Canvas Stores	
		13	Visited 167 168 & 169 VIII Inf. Bde	
		14	Short of Ingrams at 167 Bde also a shortage on 2 Machine Guns	
		15	Routine	

Army Form C. 2118.

D.A.D.O.S.,
56th DIVISION.

WAR DIARY
or
INTELLIGENCE SUMMARY.
(Erase heading not required.)

Place	Date	Hour	Summary of Events and Information	Remarks and references to Appendices
Monchecourt	Apl 16		Inspected M.S. Bn Transport Lines	
	17		Visited Supplies Kit dump in search of Divisional Signs	
	18		Visited Railhead	
	19		Stores Workshops inspected by D.A.D.M.S	
	20		Inspected Anti Gas Stores Equipment	
	21		Stores Workshops inspected by A.A. & D.M.S	
	22		Inspected & Witnessed of 168 Inf Bde units	
	23		Visited Corps Salvage Depot	
	24		Visited Leave Park	
	25		Visited by A.D.O.S. XVII Corps. Visited Railhead	
	26		Local purchases in Doullens. Prevost, St Pol & Aubigny	
	27		Routine	
	28			
	29		Inspection of 168 M.G.Coy Bn travelling Kitchens	
	30		Inspection of 167 169 A.Bde travelling Kitchens	

Army Form C. 2118.

WAR DIARY
or
INTELLIGENCE SUMMARY.
(Erase heading not required.)

D.A.D.O.S.,
56th DIVISION.

No. ....
Date. ....

Instructions regarding War Diaries and Intelligence Summaries are contained in F. S. Regs., Part II. and the Staff Manual respectively. Title pages will be prepared in manuscript.

Place	Date	Hour	Summary of Events and Information	Remarks and references to Appendices
Montescourt	May			
	1		Routine	
	2		"	
	3		Visited workshops	
	4		Inspected MG Coy transport etc. to be sent away late	
	5		"	
	6		Visited Advanced and XV Corps troops	
	7		Units & workshops inspected by DADOS	
	8		Routine	
	9		Visited by DDOS XV Corps	
	10		Inspected workshops & units of 56th Div	
	11		" " " " "	
	12		Routine	
	13		Inspected SAA returns MGC etc.	
	14		" " to 1 "	
	15		" " to 2 "	
	16		Routine	

Army Form C. 2118.

D.A.D.O.S.
36th DIVISION.

WAR DIARY
or
INTELLIGENCE SUMMARY.
(Erase heading not required.)

Instructions regarding War Diaries and Intelligence Summaries are contained in F.S. Regs., Part II. and the Staff Manual respectively. Title pages will be prepared in manuscript.

Place	Date	Hour	Summary of Events and Information	Remarks and references to Appendices
Montenescourt	May 17		Visited Railhead	
	18		Cook Lectures at Liencourt	
	19		Visited Gas 1st Division Box & Pillery Lorry area	
	20		Routine	
	21		Inspected M.T. Transport Horses. Inspection by D.D.	
	22		Inspection Mot Transport Horses	
	23		Visited by AD.O.S VIII Corps	
	24		Routine	
	25		Inspected 16g Bde Transport	
	26		Routine	
	27		Visited Gun Park & Mobile Workshops	
	28		Visited Railhead. Dump inspected by A.D.O.S	
	29		Routine	
	30		Routine	
	31		Return of 1st Blankets by all units	

Army Form C. 2118.

D.A.D.O.S.,
36th DIVISION.

WAR DIARY
or
INTELLIGENCE SUMMARY.
(Erase heading not required.)

Instructions regarding War Diaries and Intelligence Summaries are contained in F. S. Regs., Part II. and the Staff Manual respectively. Title pages will be prepared in manuscript.

Place	Date	Hour	Summary of Events and Information	Remarks and references to Appendices
Montenescourt	June 1		Routine	
	2		Inspected 169 & 164 Fld Ambulances alp	
	3		Local purchases in Aubigny, Boulogne	
	4		Stores inspected by Asst Dr Army	
	5		Routine	
	6		Inspected 169 Fld transport	
	7		Visited by army VIII Corps	
	8		Routine	
	9		Inspected 167 Fld transport	
	10		Visited by army VIII Corps	
	11		Inspected suggested type of hank supermountry	
	12		Visited Railhead, Gun Park, D.A.D.O.S Dpo Tps	
	13		Inspected 166 Fld transport. Invited by army VIII Corps	
	14		Local purchase at Boulogne at times.	
	15		Inspection of 165 Fld & tr Stores & transport	
	16		" " S.A.A.	

Army Form C. 2118.

D.A.D.O.S.,
56th DIVISION.

No............
Date............

WAR DIARY
or
INTELLIGENCE SUMMARY.
(Erase heading not required.)

Instructions regarding War Diaries and Intelligence Summaries are contained in F. S. Regs., Part II. and the Staff Manual respectively. Title pages will be prepared in manuscript.

Place	Date 1918	Hour	Summary of Events and Information	Remarks and references to Appendices
Monchiesnel	June 17		Visited by word VII Corps	
	18		Routine	
	19		Inspected the shops transport	
	20		Visited Railhead saw top [illegible]	
	21		Routine	
	22		Visited [illegible] Indian R.A.O. Workshops	
	23		Routine	
	24		Inspected M.T. Sec 4/4 & 5/1 held by shops	
	25		Visited Railhead	
	26		Inspected Reg't Rifle stores	
	27		Routine	
	28		Issued [illegible] Summary of Record	
	29		Visited [illegible] of [illegible]	
	30		Routine	

WAR DIARY or INTELLIGENCE SUMMARY.

Army Form C. 2118

D.A.D.O.S., 56th DIVISION.

Place	Date	Hour	Summary of Events and Information	Remarks and references to Appendices
Monchecourt July	1		Routine	
	2		Visited 1/5 Cheshires	
	3		Visited 169 Bde HQrs. convoi	
	4		Routine	
	5		Visited 169 Bde convoi	
	6		Conference at Corps	
	7		Visited Rum Dump	
	8		Routine	
	9		Visited Railhead	
	10		Prospecting for new dump	
	11		Routine	
	12		Preparations for moving to new dump	
	13		Move	
Villers-Sir-Simon	14			
Roellecourt	15		Weather now	
do	16		Visited Railhead	

Army Form C. 2118.

D.A.D.Q.S.,
56th DIVISION.

WAR DIARY
or
INTELLIGENCE SUMMARY.
(Erase heading not required.)

Instructions regarding War Diaries and Intelligence Summaries are contained in F. S. Regs., Part II. and the Staff Manual respectively. Title pages will be prepared in manuscript.

Place	Date	Hour	Summary of Events and Information	Remarks and references to Appendices
Rollencourt	July	17	Preparations for move to Mingoval	
Mingoval	"	18	Move	
"	"	19	Visited 167 Bde coys	
"	"	20	Visited A.D.N. Gun Park, Incident 169th coys	
"	"	21	Inspected Salvage dump	
"	"	22	Visited the Rifle ranges area	
"	"	23	Routine	
"	"	24	Visited 169 Bde	
"	"	25	Visited 80 Bde coys 1/3 Lan & Hus. & 7th American Div	
"	"	26	Visited 2/3 FMA Amb	
"	"	27	Routine	
"	"	28	Inspected field coys transport	
"	"	29	Visited ADS coys 1/3 Hus. 4 Corps Troops	
"	"	30	Visited 2.55 Workshop	
"	"	31	Commenced moving to Montreavoix	

Army Form C. 2118.

WAR DIARY
or
INTELLIGENCE SUMMARY.
(Erase heading not required.)

D.A.D.O.S.
56th DIVISION.
No...........
Date...........

Instructions regarding War Diaries and Intelligence Summaries are contained in F. S. Regs., Part II. and the Staff Manual respectively. Title pages will be prepared in manuscript.

Place	Date	Hour	Summary of Events and Information	Remarks and references to Appendices
MONTENESCOURT	Aug 1918	1	Finished march	
	"	2	Parked	
	"	3	Inspected SAA transport wagons	
	"	4	Visited 167 Bde amm	
	"	5	Visited App. to Army forge	
	"	6	Visited Railhead	
	"	7	"	
	"	8	Visited Divisional hospital & Wd Dump	
	"	9	Printers	
	"	10	Visited AAA, Lumps, & AR & heavy	
	"	11	To ADOS & DADOS 55th Div	
	"	12	Routine	
	"	13	Inspected Equipment PLE	
	"	14	Machine returns to army	
	"	15	Waiting authority to move & draw	
	"	16	Moved to Aubigny	

Army Form C. 2118.

D.A.D.O.S. 56th DIVISION.
No. ....
Date ....

WAR DIARY
or
INTELLIGENCE SUMMARY.
(Erase heading not required.)

Instructions regarding War Diaries and Intelligence Summaries are contained in F.S. Regs., Part II. and the Staff Manual respectively. Title pages will be prepared in manuscript.

Place	Date	Hour	Summary of Events and Information	Remarks and references to Appendices
Aubigny	Aug 17 1918		Move out of L.D.	Apx
"	18		Inspected Edinburgh R.E. Transport.	Apx
"	19		Visited R.H.Q.	Apx
"	20		Routine	Apx
"	21		Preparing to move to Bavincourt. Commenced moving to Bavincourt.	No car available for inspection of units going to movements of troops.
Bavincourt	22		Delivered Artex stores to all units in Division	Apx
"	" 23		Completed move. Visited by A.D.O.S. VI Corps.	Apx
"	24		Routine	Apx
"	25		Commenced moving to Bellacourt	Apx
Bellacourt	26		Completed move	Apx
"	27		Raiders visits	Apx
Boisleux Mont	28		Routine. Visited by A.D.O.S. XVII Corps.	Apx
"	29		"	
"	30		Visited A.D.O.S. Corps Salvage Dump & Gun Park.	
"	31		Routine	

Rushes Major O.B.O.S.

WAR DIARY or INTELLIGENCE SUMMARY

Army Form C. 2118.

D.A.D.O.S., 56th DIVISION.

Place	Date	Hour	Summary of Events and Information	Remarks and references to Appendices
Auchin-en-Mont	1918 Sept 1		Moved Adv Gun Park	
	" 2		" Authead	
	" 3		16.7-8-9 Bde	
	" 4		Routine	
	" 5		Visited Gun Park No 1. Railhead. Road Purches in Legrand	
	" 6		Inspection of 1/5 Cheshires transport etc	
	" 7		Preparations for moving	
St Servins Anovs	" 8		Moved. Offices to St Servins Anovs, dump to bivoary dump St Servins	
	" 9		Routine	
	" 10		Visited Adv XVIIth Corps Railhead Gun Park	
	" 11		Inspection of N.I. Sect 56 Div harness saddlery vehicles	
	" 12		Visited 1/5 Cheshires where transport	
	" 13		Routine	
	" 14		Visited y/ London R. Ambulance store transhed	
	" 15		" 7/3 "	
	" 16		Inspected Hq Rde transport & visited Rde Headquarters	

D.A.D.O.S., Army Form C. 2118.
56th DIVISION.

No. .... Date ....

WAR DIARY
or
INTELLIGENCE SUMMARY.
(Erase heading not required.)

Instructions regarding War Diaries and Intelligence Summaries are contained in F. S. Regs., Part II. and the Staff Manual respectively. Title pages will be prepared in manuscript.

Place	Date	Hour	Summary of Events and Information	Remarks and references to Appendices
St Omer	Sept 17		Visited DAC stores Arquespoint	
Omer	18		Routine	
	19		Visited Rubrout & arranged R.P.	
	20		Visited by asst XVII Corps	
	21		Visited 168 Bde stores	
	22		Visited Sun park M.I.	
	23		Routine. Receipt of blankets	
	24		Visited workshops XVII Corps	
	25		Inspected 2/1 Edin 1/3 Ldn 1/5 Cheshires 1/5 Wickshires 56 Ind Bn	
	26		" 1st & 13th & 14th London, 4th & 5th Cheshires	
	27		Routine	
	28		Inspection of Inf. mm stores	
	29		Inspection 1/69 Bde trans refitting stops latrines	
	30		Inspections for move to Nielles Lonprevent	

J Humphreys
Major
DADOS 56 Div

Army Form C. 2118.

D.A.D.O.S.,
58th DIVISION.

WAR DIARY
or
INTELLIGENCE SUMMARY.
(Erase heading not required.)

Place	Date	Hour	Summary of Events and Information	Remarks and references to Appendices
Villers-bry Agincourt	Oct 1		Visited unexpected London stores	
	2		" " " "	
	3		1/5 "	
	4		1/2 " w/ field by "	
	5		Routine	
	6		Visited Railhead (Berg)	
	7		Sun Post (Noir)	
	8		Visited 3rd 6th cars orders cases	
	9		Routine	
	10		Visited 167 Bde stores	
	11		" 3/ Rets & Rcd stores	
	12		Routine	
	13		Visited Adm. to Pk & Bn !	
	14		Preparations for moving	
	15		Moved to Mareuil	
Mareuil	16		Routine	

Army Form C. 2118.

WAR DIARY
or
INTELLIGENCE SUMMARY.
(Erase heading not required.)

Place	Date	Hour	Summary of Events and Information	Remarks and references to Appendices
Murand	Oct 1918	17	Receipt of Winter clothing	
		18	Inspected Clean clothes store	
		19	Visited Gun Pit.	
		20	Visited Railhead	
		21	Visited 56 Div A.T. Coy stores	
		22	Inspected 7 Mex Stores	
		23	Routine	
		24	Visited Coy Hd. Qtrs	
		25		
		26	Visited New Coy	
		27	Routine	
		28	Local Purchases in tourni	
		29	Preparation for move to Treswille	
Treswille		30	Moved Office & Dumps	
		31		

Army Form C. 2118.

D.A.D.O.S.,
56th DIVISION.

WAR DIARY
or
INTELLIGENCE SUMMARY.
(Erase heading not required.)

Place	Date	Hour	Summary of Events and Information	Remarks and references to Appendices
Avesnelle	Nov 1/18	1	Routine	
		2	Visited Railhead. Nothing on car	
		3	Visited Headquarters — No cars available	
		4	Routine	
		5	Went to men to Carlepont	
Caullery		6	Move to Valenciennes. No accommodation at Carlepont	
Newson		7	Routine	
		8	Visited Railway	
		9	Interviewed for move	
Ant le Franc		10	J. Manning Ambulance	
Nangis		11		
		12	Routine	
		13	Inspected the Rifle Store	
		14	Inspected the Rifle Store	
		15	Inspected "67 RAC" Workshops	
		16	Routine	

Army Form C. 2118.

WAR DIARY
or
INTELLIGENCE SUMMARY.
(Erase heading not required.)

Place	Date	Hour	Summary of Events and Information	Remarks and references to Appendices
Blangy	Apr 17			
		18		
		19	Great Improvement	
		20		
		21		
		22		
		23		
		24		
		25	Routine	
		26		
		27	Instructions for moving	
ASQUILLIES		28	Move	
		29	Routine	
		30	Routine	

Army Form C. 2118.

WAR DIARY
or
INTELLIGENCE SUMMARY.
(Erase heading not required.)

Instructions regarding War Diaries and Intelligence Summaries are contained in F. S. Regs., Part II. and the Staff Manual respectively. Title pages will be prepared in manuscript.

Place	Date	Hour	Summary of Events and Information	Remarks and references to Appendices
Aspidiha dismbd	1918	1	[illegible]	
		2	[illegible]	
		3	[illegible]	
		4	[illegible]	
		5	[illegible]	
		6	[illegible]	
		7	[illegible]	
		8	[illegible]	
		9	[illegible]	
		10	[illegible]	
		11	[illegible]	
		12	[illegible]	
		13	[illegible]	
		14	[illegible]	
		15	[illegible]	

WAR DIARY
or
INTELLIGENCE SUMMARY.
(Erase heading not required.)

Army Form C. 2118.

D.A.D.O.S.,
56th DIVISION.

Place	Date	Hour	Summary of Events and Information	Remarks and references to Appendices
Agnelleres	Oct	16	Routine	
		17	do	
		18	Inspected No. VAD Workshop Stores	
		19	513 field Coy "	
		20	Visited Lieut Col Hughes kit dump	
		21	Routine	
		22	Routine	
		23	Routine	
		24	Visited 2/3 1 Field Ambulance	
		25	Routine	
		26	Routine	
		27	Visited Aroud Section kit dump	
		28	Routine	
		29	Visited Railhead	
		30	Inspected H.W. Coy ASC Transport	
	31	Routine		

Original

War Diary

January 1919

DMDOS 36th Division

Army Form C. 2118.

WAR DIARY
or
INTELLIGENCE SUMMARY.
(Erase heading not required.)

D.A.D.O.S.
56th Div[ision]

Place	Date	Hour	Summary of Events and Information	Remarks and references to Appendices
Aguilbre	January 1919			
	1		Routine	
	2		Routine	
	3		Visited Supplies Ink Dump & 1 Londons Stores	
	4		Visited by ADOS XXII Corps - Desert Subjects inspected	
	5		Routine	
	6		Visited Divl. Bn. & inspected they Coln transport	
	7		Inspected Hy Bde Transport	
	8		Routine	
	9		Visited Railhead at Mons	
	10		Visited 1/5 th London Regt	
	11		Routine	
	12		Inspected 1st London Transport	
	13		Visited 168 Bde	
	14		Routine	
	15		Visited 1/4 th London Regt	

Army Form C. 2118.

WAR DIARY
or
INTELLIGENCE SUMMARY.
(Erase heading not required.)

Instructions regarding War Diaries and Intelligence Summaries are contained in F. S. Regs., Part II. and the Staff Manual respectively. Title pages will be prepared in manuscript.

D.A.D.O.S.
56th DIVISION.

Place	Date	Hour	Summary of Events and Information	Remarks and references to Appendices
Bapaume	Jan 16		Posted to Bde HQ	
	17		Visited ASC type & Div 67 MT workshop	
	18		Inspected 513 under of Mech transport	
	19		Inspected visited 167 168 169 Inf Workshops	
	20		Inspected transport of Rifle Brigade	
	21			
	22		Visited No 10 Coy 53 Div Train	
	23		Routine	
	24		Visited 167 Inf Bde transport	
	25		Inspection of 59 Div MG Coy lightly inspected	
	26		transport 2/2	
	27		Inspected Rifle Brigade	
	28		Visited MGC HQrs	
	29		Routine	
	30			
	31		Routine	

Original
No 31

War Diary

February 1919

D.A.D.O.S. 56th Division

Army Form C. 2118.

WAR DIARY
or
INTELLIGENCE SUMMARY.
(Erase heading not required.)

Instructions regarding War Diaries and Intelligence Summaries are contained in F. S. Regs., Part II. and the Staff Manual respectively. Title pages will be prepared in manuscript.

Place	Date	Hour	Summary of Events and Information	Remarks and references to Appendices
Napier[?]	1919	1	Routine	
		2	Visited by Very RE Base train	
		3	" "	
		4	Routine	
		5	Visited R.E. to log HQ	
		6	Routine	
		7	Visited B.G.H. Good [illeg.]	
		8	Routine	
		9	Visited Stables R/ dumps	
		10	Army XIII Corps	
		11	Visited 4th London divn	
		12	Routine	
		13	Inspected 4th London divn	
		14	Visited Army – 4 met Army	
		15	" Col. Y Nast	
		16	Routine	

Army Form C. 2118.

D.A.D.O.S.
56th DIVISION.

WAR DIARY
or
INTELLIGENCE SUMMARY.
(Erase heading not required.)

Instructions regarding War Diaries and Intelligence Summaries are contained in F. S. Regs., Part II. and the Staff Manual respectively. Title pages will be prepared in manuscript.

Place	Date	Hour	Summary of Events and Information	Remarks and references to Appendices
Bapaume	Sept 1917	17	Posted to 1st Army	
		18	Rothem	
		19	Conference at Corps	
		20	Routine	
		21	Posted WADN to Division	
		22	" " 51st "	
		23	Routine	
		24	"	
		25	Posted M to Corps Tps	
		26	Posted WADN XIII Corps	
		27	Inspected Divnl area	
		28	Routine	

Vol 38

Original

D.A.D.O.S.
56th Division

War Diary

March 1919

Army Form C.2118

WAR DIARY
or
INTELLIGENCE SUMMARY
(Erase heading not required.)

Instructions regarding War Diaries and Intelligence Summaries are contained in F.S. Regs., Part II. and the Staff Manual respectively. Title Pages will be prepared in manuscript.

D.A.D.V.S., 55th DIVISION.
No..........
Date..........

Place	Date	Hour	Summary of Events and Information	Remarks and references to Appendices
Aquillies	Mar	1	Rendent 1st London	
		2	Inspected Regt stores	
		3	Inspected 1/5 Middlesex transport horses	
		4	Rendent	
		5	Visited Railhead	
		6	Visited ADVS XVII Corps	
		7	Visited farriers in search of new lamp	
		8	Rendent	
		9	Inspected 1/5 The J. Ambulance	
		10	Rendent	
		11	Visited A.D.V.S. XVII Corps	
		12	Visited 104 Battery re demobilisation	
		13		
		14	Visited Railhead	
		15	Gonzure	
		16	Inspected 1/5 London Regt transport & horses	

1875 Wt. W593/826 1,000,000 4/15 J.B.C. & A. A.D.S.S./Forms/C.2118.

WAR DIARY or INTELLIGENCE SUMMARY

Army Form C. 2118

(Erase heading not required.)

Place	Date	Hour	Summary of Events and Information	Remarks and references to Appendices
Asquillies	Apr 18		Visited A.D. 22nd Corps troops approx	
	19		Visited arrangements for Field Punish'd Office	
			Bureau	
	19		Bureau	
	20		Visited troops Salvage Punish approx	
	21		Visited by A.D.M.S. 32nd Corps	
	22		Inspected Horse & Transport of 36th Div Signal Coy	
	23		Jenlain	
	24		Inspected 166 Inf Bde	
	25		Inspected 167 Inf Bde	
	26		Inspected 169 Inf Bde	
	27		Inspected 56th D.A.C. & 281 Bde R.F.A.	
	28		" 281 Bde R.F.A.	
	29		513 " 708 A.C. R.F.A.	
Jenlain	30		Inspected 216 & 512 Field Coys	
	31		56 R.E. M.	

WAR DIARY
or
INTELLIGENCE SUMMARY

Army Form C. 2

(Erase heading not required.)

Instructions regarding War Diaries and Intelligence Summaries are contained in F. S. Regs., Part II. and the Staff Manual respectively. Title Pages will be prepared in manuscript.

Place	Date	Hour	Summary of Events and Information	Remarks and references to Appendices
Jonghe Afqueu	Apl 19	1	Inspected 8th Signal Co	
		2	Inspected 6th Do M.G.K. train	
		3	Went round refuses much simplify	
		4	Shoeing of carts, contents & eqpt	
		5	Inspected 1st London Regt RAMC	
		6	Routine	
		7	Inspected 27th Infy	
		8	" 53rd Do	
		9	Routine	
		10	Inspected Hq T.M.B	
		11	" 1/6 th London Regt	
		12	Routine	
		13	Routine	
		14	Commenced the additional duties of sanitation	
		15	Inspected 58 M.G.C.	
		16	Routine	

Army Form C.2118

WAR DIARY
or
INTELLIGENCE SUMMARY

(Erase heading not required.)

Instructions regarding War Diaries and Intelligence Summaries are contained in F.S. Regs., Part II. and the Staff Manual respectively. Title Pages will be prepared in manuscript.

D.A.D.O.S.,
39th DIVISION.

Place	Date	Hour	Summary of Events and Information	Remarks and references to Appendices
Zenghis Kl. Rgren	17		Visited Rutkead 63 Div	
	18		do	
	19		Holiday	
	20			
	21		Routine	
	22		Visited & inspected Store of Div from 63rd Div	
	23		Visited H.S. Appis	
	24		Visited D.S.O.S. No 1 Area	
	25		Routine	
	26		Inspected Store of Drake Batt 63rd Div	
	27		Visited A.B.O.S. 1 Area Landas & Sub-Area Dublin	
	28		Inspected Stores of Field Ambulances & Batts 63rd Div	
	29		Routine & Sub-Area work	
	30			

Murhuye Major

1875 Wt. W593/826 1,000,000 4/15 J.B.C. & A. A.D.S.S./Forms/C. 2118.

WAR DIARY
or
INTELLIGENCE SUMMARY

(Erase heading not required.)

Army Form C. 2118

BERTUS 56 / Vol 40

Place	Date	Hour	Summary of Events and Information	Remarks and references to Appendices
Jerusalem	1919 May			
	1		Visited Jerusalem and Jaffa Sub Area	
	2		Routine & visited 63rd Division	
	3		Routine & 63rd Division	
	4		Visited I.G.S. Jaffa & Jaffa Sub-Area	
	5		Routine	
	6		Visited 63rd Divn & Jaffa Sub-Area	
	7		Routine	
	8		Visited by ADMS	
	9		Routine	
	10		Visited Jerusalem & Jaundry	
	11		Visited I.G.S. Jaffa	
	12		Routine	
	13		Inspected Units prior to Entrainment	
	14		Routine	
	15		Inspected Units prior to Entrainment	
	16		Jerusalem & Jaffa Sub Area	
	17		Routine	
	18		Visited Units prior to Entrainment	
	19		Routine	
	20		Routine	

Army Form C. 2118

WAR DIARY
or
INTELLIGENCE SUMMARY
(Erase heading not required.)

Instructions regarding War Diaries and Intelligence Summaries are contained in F.S. Regs., Part II. and the Staff Manual respectively. Title Pages will be prepared in manuscript.

Place	Date	Hour	Summary of Events and Information	Remarks and references to Appendices
Jerusalem	May			
	21		Visited 63rd Divn & A.C.O.	
	22		Visited A.C.O. offices	
	23		Routine	
	24		Visited by O.S.S.O. Supply Column and inspected stocks Arab Entanglements	
	25		Routine	
	26		Routine	
	27		Visited Railhead	
	28		Visited D.D.O.S. No 1 Area	
	29		Routine	
	30		Inspected Units prior to Entrainment	
	31		Routine	

Army Form C. 2118

WAR DIARY
INTELLIGENCE SUMMARY
(Erase heading not required.)

Instructions regarding War Diaries and Intelligence Summaries are contained in F.S. Regs., Part II. and the Staff Manual respectively. Title Pages will be prepared in manuscript.

NWD 8562

July 41

Place	Date Hour	Summary of Events and Information	Remarks and references to Appendices
Jonapples	June 1	Visited ADDS & Puithead	
	2	Inspected Stores of 63rd Division	
	3	Routine	
	4	Visited ISM's hospital at Obenz	
	5	Cleared Divl. Baths & Clothing	
	6	Routine	
	7	Routine	
	8	Inspected 15th Welsh Regt. prior to Entrainment	
	9	Visited 63rd Divn. Units	
	10	Visited HQs & Puithead	
	11	Routine	
	12	Inspected Stores of Drake Batt. 63 Divn.	
	13	Routine	
	14	Stores visited by ADDS typres Lardres	
	15	Supervised handing in of Stores by 282 Bn.	
	16	ditto	
	17	Routine	
	18	Visited 63rd Division	
	19	Visited Puithead & HDS	

Army Form C. 2118

WAR DIARY
INTELLIGENCE SUMMARY
(Erase heading not required.)

Instructions regarding War Diaries and Intelligence Summaries are contained in F. S. Regs., Part II. and the Staff Manual respectively. Title Pages will be prepared in manuscript.

Place	Date	Hour	Summary of Events and Information	Remarks and references to Appendices
Gnaphos	1919 Feb. C			
	20		Visited D Bos HQ 1 am	
	21		RAoS Apns lathes vested Store	
	22		Practice	
	23		Supervised loading in of stores from hd q 63rd Divn	
	24		— ditto —	
	25		Practice & visited 63rd Divn Ordnance	
	26		Visited 63rd Division Hdts	
	27		Inspected Ordnance Stores at General Dump Apns	
	28		Jouten	
	29		Practice & Band K.O.S	
	30		Visited Lowland and Apns R.O.S	

www.ingramcontent.com/pod-product-compliance
Lightning Source LLC
Chambersburg PA
CBHW081431160426
43193CB00013B/2254